SANDPLAY

SANDPLAY /

Sigo Press

Dora M. Kalff

A Psychotherapeutic Approach
to the Psyche

SIGO PRESS
2601 Ocean Park Blvd., #210, Santa Monica, CA. 90405

ISNB 0-93843400-4

Translation of Sandspiel.
Bibliography: p. 169
1. Play therapy. 2. Art therapy. 3. Sand tables
—Therapeutic use. 4. Child psychotherapy—Case
studies. 5. Psychotherapy—Case studies. I. Title.
RJ505.P6K313 1980   618.92'891653   80-27195

First revised edition produced and edited by Sisa Sternback-Scott with the help of Rochelle Wallace. Manufactured by Peace Press for SIGO.

Original translation by Hilde Kirsch
Translation for first revised edition by Wendayne Ackerman

Book Design by Sisa Sternback-Scott
Cover Design John Coy

To my sons and grandson
Peter Baudouin
Martin Michael
Christopher Baudouin

CONTENTS

PROLOGUE

I feel indeed privileged to have been asked to write the prologue for Mrs. Kalff's most important book. I would like to begin by telling you a story, a fairy tale. It is a story that is most appropriate to the content of the author's book, as well as to the author herself, for it deals with the thread of inner life that exemplifies Mrs. Kalff as a person, as a therapist, and as a writer.

There was once a lovely young princess whose name was Irene. Her father was a very good king who spent much of his time among the people of his kingdom, trying to do everything he could to help them in any way he could. Irene's mother died when she was very young, and so she had no memory of her.

For long periods of time, Irene lived in a special castle in the country where she was cared for by an elderly maid and a retinue of servants who took care of the castle and guarded it. Irene stayed here because the father was gone so often from the main castle, attending to the affairs of state.

What the King did not know was that the country home was built on a mountain beneath which lived goblins who were very unfriendly to the King; and they had a plan to steal the princess and marry her to the goblin prince.

Irene had a friend, her only friend, who lived in a very poor home not too far from where the castle was located. His name was Curdie, and he worked in the coal mines and was the son of a coal miner. You will hear more about Curdie soon.

The castle that Irene lived in was very large. She was allowed to roam the front part of the castle at will but was instructed that she must never open a certain door because it led into the back regions of the castle where one could very easily become lost. Needless to say, like the proper heroine she was, one day she opened the door and began to explore all the multitude of rooms she found on the upper and lower levels. After a few hours, she became confused, lost in a maze, and began to cry. Like the proper princess she was, however, she soon got control of herself and began again to search for a way back to the main part of the castle.

She came to yet another door which she opened; and there, to her great amazement, sat a woman in the middle of the room, spinning at a spinning wheel. Irene was absolutely amazed. I am sure that you would be amazed, too, if you opened a door and found such a figure spinning away at her wheel. And wouldn't you be more amazed yet if the figure stopped, looked up at you, said, "Hello," and then told you that she had been waiting for you to come for a long time?

Well, that is exactly what happened. Irene, of course, was very surprised at this and asked the woman who she was. Then came the biggest surprise, for the woman told her that she was her grandmother.

Now this was a bit of a shock to Irene. In the first place, she did not know that she had a grandmother. In the second place, this woman was as old as old can be, older than any grandmother could be; and she was, at the same time, as young and beautiful as any woman can be.

Irene walked over to the grandmother and told her that she did not even know she had a grandmother. The woman answered that everyone has a grandmother — only some know it and some do not; that it was only a question of seeing what's there.

Princess Irene walked over to the spinning wheel and watched the grandmother spin. She looked at the thread, but it was so fine she could not even see it. She asked the grandmother what she was making; and the grandmother told her that she was making a special gift, just for her, and that it would soon be ready, but it was not yet the time. She told Irene it was best that she leave now, but to come back again in a few days, and that it was best, really, to keep the visit secret.

Irene left the grandmother and found her way back to the main rooms of the castle. She got a good scolding from her old maid servant about being away so long, but she kept the secret well and said nothing about her explorations.

In the succeeding weeks, Princess Irene visited her grandmother often. She loved to sit and talk to her and watch her spin her invisible thread. One day she told her friend Curdie that she wanted to share something with him which was very special, and she told him about the grandmother and took him to see her. When they entered the room, Irene introduced Curdie to her grandmother and her grandmother to Curdie.

Curdie stood there, looking around the room, staring rather vacantly, and obviously getting angrier and angrier. Finally, he took his miner's hat and threw it to the floor; he yelled at Irene that if this was her idea of a joke, he was having none of it! With this, he stomped out of the room in a great rage, furious at Irene for the trick she had played on him.

Irene, as you can imagine, was heartbroken, and she began sobbing. As you have probably guessed, Curdie could not see the grandmother. She was invisible to him. After Irene regained her composure, the grandmother told Irene that she had to realize that not everyone could see her and that she must not rush people who were unable to do so. In his own time, she pointed out, Curdie would be able to see her, for it was his fate to do so. Then the grandmother told Irene that on the following night she was to return; at that time her very special gift would be ready and the spinning done.

Irene was a very excited young lady, and she could hardly contain her excitement until the next night. It finally came, however, and Irene went to the room on this very special night. The grandmother undressed her and bathed her in a very special water. Then she dressed her in a very special gown, and Irene was ready for the gift.

The grandmother took out the ball of yarn she had been working on for such a long time. First she put the ball of yarn in her drawer; then, drawing out the end of it, she handed it to Irene.

You may imagine the surprise—and the disappointment—of the young princess when she realized that she could not even see the thread. The grandmother was not at all surprised at Irene's discomfiture. She told her then that it was certainly true one could not see this thread; that it was, indeed, invisible. However, one could feel it; one could only feel it.

Irene then expressed her second disappointment. She wanted to know what kind of gift this was which stayed in the grandmother's drawer. It was bad enough that the thread was invisible, but it made no sense at all to be given a gift she could not have, one which was to be kept in the grandmother's drawer.

The grandmother told her it would be no gift at all if the ball were any place but with her. She told Irene that she must take this thread and carry it with her wherever she went. Then, whenever she was in difficulty or need, all she had to do was follow it back to its source and this would enable her to find her way out of danger.

Irene was a bit mystified by all this: A gift which was invisible, one she could not see but could only feel, a gift which was kept in her grandmother's room, while she had only its end. She was mystified, and yet she also knew that something very important had been given to her, and she left the grandmother. You may be sure the time came when she was in great danger, when the gift of the grandmother was something she very much appreciated having as well as something she learned to understand.

At this point, however, we leave the adventures of Princess Irene and her grandmother, and you may read and follow these adventures in detail by reading George McDonald's beautiful fairy-tale novel, *The Princess and the Goblins.* As I mentioned in my first paragraph, I have chosen to use the beginning of this tale to introduce Mrs. Kalff's most important book, because it is so appropriate to the issues in it and, in some special way, to the author herself. Let me first, however, deal with some of the critical issues of our time so that we may see Mrs. Kalff's work in perspective.

We live in an age of revolution, a revolution of the unconscious, which is destroying old forms and often has nothing to substitute for the old ways but chaotic energy. We are reaping the harvest of centuries of repression of the unconscious. Western Man has long since destroyed his Gods and substituted in their places the God of Reason and Rationality. Imagination has been lost. Emotions have been negated. Dreams have become a forgotten language. Demons have been ruled out of existence, Evil has been consigned to the metaphysical constructs of the Middle Ages. We, all of us, are both the victims and the processors of this brand of insanity, and today we are all paying the piper. The unconscious is in revolt against its oppressor; namely, rational consciousness as it has been known over the past few centuries.

Some years ago, I worked with a woman who suffered from severe migraine headaches. We had worked through many problems and areas of conflict, but the migraines remained until the appearance of a particular dream. The headaches did not disappear because of the dream. Rather, a change was going on in the unconscious that led to the dream and to the disappearance of the symptom. This is a noncausal view, a view that C. G. Jung has termed synchronistic.

In her dream, the patient was cleaning out her medicine cabinet, throwing away old bottles. Then she found two small and very old bottles which she took out and looked at. To her amazement, each bottle had a small snake in it, and each bottle was labeled 1385, signifying the year that the snake was bottled. She knew she had to let the snakes out, fearful though she was. She went outside and opened one of the bottles, and the snake crawled out and went down into a gully. A while later, it came back up; it was larger, had appendages, and it went off into nature.

Symptomatically, the patient's migraine disappeared; and, behaviorally, there was released an expression of emotion that had been held in before. The question for us concerns the year of the bottling. The year 1385 is really at the start of the whole development of scientific humanism. Coming out of the Middle Ages, when the individual was immersed in the unconscious, in magic, in superstition and fear centering around the Catholic Church, scientific humanism was like a breath of fresh air. It promised knowledge and the release of man from the prison of medieval fantasies. The problem is that it went too far. The development of the mind, of knowledge, of a scientific approach to life and life's problems was at the expense of the bottling of the snake and at the expense of the containment of the snake with its manifold symbolic meanings. The snake expresses primitive emotion. It expresses sexuality. It expresses the whole realm of the imagination that became consigned to an increasingly inferior position as we moved more and more into our scientific age.

The release of the snake was not just a personal problem for this patient. It is a historical problem which involves each of us, for we are, all of us, born into the world with two histories: the personal, familiar one and an impersonal, collective one.

To summarize then, humanism brought mankind out of the Middle Ages. It brought us into a new kind of relationship to our fellow man, but it also began a movement of the mind away from the unconscious. This movement of the conscious and unconscious away from each other has continued until fairly recent times; but today, at the start of the decade of "the 70's," we see the curve changing and a movement taking place which I hope will bring the conscious and unconscious into a close enough relationship in the coming generations so that a bridge may be built between them. Certainly this is the challenge for each individual.

Energies are pouring through and out of us in so many different ways. We see them in wars, in rioting, in black-white confrontation. We see people, youngsters, gulping pills so that they can "feel" things, so that they can see visions. We find psychologists trying to find new ways to cope with energy. Encounter groups and sensitivity-training groups are ways of trying to help people get to their repressed feelings and emotions, though there is often a total unawareness that they are dealing with the unconscious in these efforts.

There are the traditional psychotherapeutic systems which are concerned with the general issues of healing. Here we see a most remarkable shift of emphasis taking place. The beginning of psychiatry was marked by a concern with symptoms and their removal. What has been developing more and more in recent years is a developmental outlook to these very same problems. These growth-centered approaches are concerned with the overall development of personality. Symptoms are expressions of a life style which is wrong in some way: It is too constricted; there is blockage to certain energy systems. Personality is seen as having in it a capacity for growth and healing that needs to be freed and allowed to grow and evolve.

Depth psychology has, of course, always espoused the cause of the healing function of the psyche. The work of C. G. Jung caught the imagination of many professionals because he spoke of modern man's separation from his soul. He spoke of the necessity of modern man connecting to the spirit within in order to bring meaning again to our lives and to end the terrible rat race of modern living. There are many today who speak to this end. One can no longer speak of schools of psychology as though one has the truth of the spirit and another one does not. There are creative pscyhotherapists who are open to both inner and outer life, and there are those who are not. Mrs. Kalff is such a creative psychotherapist, a Jungian analyst by training, a free spirit in living, and in this book she brings us an expression of her very individual way of dealing with the issue of personality development, for her approach goes far beyond the question of making sick people well.

Mrs. Kalff brings us a way of objectifying, in the form of symbols, the energy of the unconscious, through the medium of sandplay. This creative evolution of symbolic expression is encouraged to evolve in the child or adult in as free and untrammeled a way as is possible. The effect is healing in the traditional sense, but, even more importantly, it leads to the deepest connection to the center within which is the source of the human spirit.

The sandbox is not an instrument of magic. It is a tool, an extremely effective tool, for getting to the imagination and allowing it to become creative. But it is more than a tool. It is also an expression of the therapist, as a creative personality, who relates to patients both personally and symbolically at an extremely deep level. The symbolic evolution one observes in these cases does not just occur in the vacuum of the sandbox and therapy room. It occurs in the presence of Mrs. Kalff who provides a *temenos,* a receptive container, in which the deepest emotions and expressions of phantasy have a chance to manifest themselves and be received, appreciated, and understood. The unconscious knows a friend, and Mrs. Kalff is a friend to the unconscious as well as to the patient himself.

The great need of our time is for people to be connected to spirit; for people to be connected to a core of feeling in themselves that makes their lives vital and full of meaning, that makes life a mystery evermore to be uncovered. Our dreams help us to connect to this mystery. Meditation, for many people, provides access to the depths of our inner being. The sandbox provides us with access to these innermost feeling cores and permits a process to be set into motion which has as its hopeful result a connection to the invisible thread of Princess Irene. Her thread is one that cannot be seen; it can only be felt. And so it is with the intangible thread of the human spirit. It cannot be seen; it can only be felt.

But how are we to feel it in these days of constant activity, roaring traffic, noise, smog, unrest, and violence? We must develop ways of helping ourselves and; if we are therapists, of helping the patient to connect his conscious ego to his deeper feeling center, to that eternal center of spirit which has always been the core and sustenance of man. This is why the grand-mother's gift must be kept in her drawer. The invisible thread of spirit is rooted in a spiritual center; what Jung has called the Self or the objective psyche; what Maslow has called the biological basis of the psyche. It is being connected to this center which is the great gift of the grandmother to Irene.

Western culture has become a deadly affair so far as helping people to reach this center by ordinary means. School has become a deadly affair, and only now are there the first glimmerings of changes on the horizon. Education has become the instrument by which we have perpetuated the destruction of the human spirit. Our aim has been to make children conform as quickly as possible, to begin thinking and learning as quickly as possible, to compete against their classmates for grades and recognition—all of which effectively destroys the development of an intrinsic desire to learn.

We destroy in ourselves the ability to play, to have fun. It is no accident that the new ethic among young people today has to do with "being" and "playing" rather than doing. Thinking so much, we have forgotten how to play; particularly, how to allow the play of imagination and phantasy. We have lost our connection to story telling, to fable and myth, for this is another form of play with our imagination. Play is a very fundamental and necessary hunger of children and adults. The connection to play is the connection to phantasy, and it is essential that play and phantasy have a chance to operate in our lives, for they are central avenues by which the ego contacts, and stays in contact with, the deep reservoir of imagery we call the Self.

One of the reasons why the sandbox is such an effective tool is that it provides us with the chance to play. For many adults, it is the first time they remember ever being able to play. It is sad to see a youngster of ten and realize that the only time during the week he has the opportunity to allow his imagination free rein is while he is playing in the sandbox during his therapy hour.

We do not value imagination, which is a strange thing when you consider the amount of time we spend in phantasy activity. It is, of course, phantasy activity of the wrong kind—daydreaming that occupies huge chunks of time and is generally uncreative. By negating imagination and emotion; by not allowing these fundamental human propensities the chance to live in us in a regular way, they become repressed. In becoming repressed, they become engorged, magnified, and increasingly negative. This is why, I believe, there are so many "monster" dreams in children today. The unconscious operates in us like a personality with whom we might be living. If we ignore this other person, he or she turns sour and turns against us. So it is with the unconscious. If we ignore it, it turns sour and turns against us.

One commonly sees in children dreams of lions or wild animals which are attacking the child. These often occur in waking states before going to sleep. Our traditional way of handling these dreams and phantasies is to reassure the child that there is nothing really there. We turn on the lights and show him "reality" to prove there is no lion under the bed or in the closet. The terrible thing is that the child is soon convinced nothing is there. Then it is "only" a dream, or it is "only" his imagination. This is a typical bit of schizophrenic insanity which is part of upbringing. I use the term schizophrenic insanity because this is how we perpetuate the split between conscious and unconscious.

What is reality? Not too long ago, in the southern California desert, a man stopped his car, leaped out, yelling all the time that the Commies were coming. He then ran into the desert where he eventually died. It was "only" his imagination, but he is a dead man because of it. Do we fear the hydrogen bomb? It is unlikely that one will go off by itself. It is "only" the imagination, the phantasies, of people who have access to these weapons we have to fear.

The lions or monsters of our children's dreams are *real*! It is a different kind of reality than we are used to dealing with, but we have to get used to this reality. There is no "right" way to deal with these dreams and phantasies. What we can say, in a definitive sense, is that they must be taken seriously by the adult. This alone will produce a change. There are also techniques one can use. One can have a child paint a picture of a lion. If the image is not too frightening, the next day the child might be asked to visualize the lion and describe it. The child might mold the image in clay or tell a story. All of these ideas are ways of taking the image seriously, and what we do will depend on the age of the child and where we are as parents.

The unconscious, we must realize, is a term which describes energy. This energy is expressed in two ways: One way is by emotion and the other by thought and image. A child must come into connection with his natural emotions, or he will not be able to live and compete with his peer group. Our culture has blunted our emotions, however, by placing a premium on "being good," or what might be better expressed as "not being bad." This has to do, no doubt, with a variety of factors, not the least of which is the system of some ideas we may term the Christian ethic. This ethic began with the deification of Christ and the Fall (expulsion) from heaven of the Archangel, Satan. The fall from heaven, in fact, tumbled him rather deeply into the unconscious of Western Man where he has lived in symbolic form, carrying the emotions and passions which gradually drained out of his counterpart in heaven.

What I am saying here is that the image of God as expressed in Jesus became too white and too light; for without the Satanic element, we have no connection to our bodies, to our emotions, or our passions. It is no accident today that we observe the amazing phenomena of witch covens, Satan worship, and black magic rituals. They are expressions of the dark side of a god image become too light.

We are faced with a situation comparable in many ways to the emergence in Greece of the god Dionysus. He came, in mythological development, as essentially an invader from the north, entering into the Greek pantheon at a relatively late date. He compensated for the god Apollo who had become too light, too structured, and too tame. Naturally, a more passionate god image needed to force its way in.

So it is that today we witness all around us the re-emergence of the Dionysian energy with all its power and fury, frenzy and passion, and life-giving energy. Our greatest challenge as individuals is to find a vessel for this energy so that we may find a harmonious balance between the structuring and the experiencing part of ourselves. The sandbox leads the child typically to a balance between his structuring and experiencing sides.

Mrs. Kalff's method with the sandbox has two parts to it: The first direction is to make the picture; after this is done, the patient is asked to tell the story. Both of these acts are extremely important. The creation of the image itself is essentially an introverted act, and I have heard Mrs. Kalff describe this as a kind of Western meditation. Eastern meditation systems tend, with some exceptions, to be imageless. Though many Westerners are drawn to these systems, it is my view that the meditation of the West will increasingly be dealing with imagery. The sandbox is one expression for this. Other expressions are what Carl Jung calls active imagination; what the psychosynthesis people call symbolic visualization; what gestaltists call guided vision; what Ira Progoff calls twilight imaging. The telling of the story is the spinning of a tale. Most youngsters like to tell the story, although, as Mrs. Kalff points out clearly in her teaching, this must never be forced.

Thus, we see that sandplay is just what the name implies. It is play in sand; play in the critical sense of imaginative freedom and experimentation, fun and fear, everything else that goes to make up the imagination. For in the imagination is contained all the positive and the highest good; all the negative and the deepest evil.

But there is an important limitation attached to this freedom of phantasy. The box is of a specific dimension. This dimension essentially allows the onlooker to view it in one glance without shifting one's head from side to side. This dimension of the box is quite critical as a factor, because it means that the total freedom of phantasy which is available to the child has a built-in limitation; namely, the size of the box. It must be a container, a *temenos,* and the very fact that the *temenos* is there enhances the child's freedom.

We live in a time when the issue of limits is a very critical one. As I have mentioned, we are now seeing the unconscious breaking through as a powerful energy system. When this kind of breakthrough takes place; when one experiences this kind of Dionysian energy after a lifetime of what feels like sterility, there is a tendency to over identify with the Dionysian impulses. This tendency to over-react is, of course, more strongly constellated in the parental figures (or surrogates or establishment) who are too stuck on the side of the image of "goodness," and/or excessive structure, and/or non-emotionality.

What this leads to, in our time, are people who feel they must express everything which is in them, as though the answer to the ills of society were a massive cathartic. There is no question about our need, individually, to loosen up, for we have indeed suffered from a state of severe repression of our emotions. Our need for expression must be tempered, however, by some feeling of responsibility towards our fellow man; otherwise, that elusive freedom we are looking for in expressing ourselves will be lost. If one has to "let it out" on the basis of an idea that this is *the* thing to do, then there is no longer freedom but rather a new dogma.

One of the phantasies of the new encounter-ethic in contemporary psychology is that it is always good to "encounter" someone—to really "let someone have it." This is just what I have called it, a phantasy. It may lead to a creative and positive human communication, or it may release the demonic contents of the unconscious in a most destructive and damaging way. This is why emotions are so often repressed. These contents have been underneath for centuries, and they sometimes need to be transformed before the individual can allow them to come out. Sandplay is one way of accomplishing this transformation of energy.

Sandplay originated with Margaret Lowenfeld in England. It was picked up in the United States by Charlotte Buhler who used it as a diagnostic agent and prepared it as an actual kit that clinicians could purchase. It was then taken up by Mrs.

Kalff whose widespread travels have started people working with the sandbox in all parts of the world.

Why have therapists taken so to this method? The reason, I think, is similar to the phenomenon one experiences if one is an observer of some ritual activity. Observers of a real ritual actually become participants, chords of deep feeling are touched, and there is a sense of identity with the group. The therapist who observes the symbolic portrayals and the verbal phantasies of sandplay becomes involved in a deeply meaningful ritual. We are affected by these symbolic portrayals, and our own symbolic life is activated. A true symbol is always experienced by the patient and by the therapist, unless the therapist insists on reducing the symbol to a purely causalistic system and thus squeezes all the juice out of it. The interest in sandplay has spread, not only because it is such an effective tool in the healing process, but also because the therapist is touched so deeply by the experience.

I remember the first time that I ever saw Mrs. Kalff's slide series. It was many years ago, and I had already been using a sandbox in my work with children—using it, though, in an interpretive way, setting up scenes, making suggestions. When I first saw Mrs. Kalff's work; when I saw the evolution of imagery in a particular child, I felt as though I had come home. Here was someone who could let a development take place, who related to the child with the deepest warmth and connection, but who could allow the symbolic life to live its own way. One becomes involved even by watching the development of these symbols on slides—let alone having the privilege of seeing them in one's office.

I must warn those of you who are therapists that the use of the sandbox is an expensive disease to catch. Once you start building sandboxes, making shelves, and, particularly, once you start buying figures, you are hopelessly ensnared in the joys of the playful child (and I hope not compulsive child, for your sake) who wants more and more toys, ostensibly for your patients to have at their disposal.

I want to emphasize again that the use of the sandbox is not a method of therapy in and of itself. It is a tool in the hands of the artist. It is a method used in therapy to objectify the contents of imagination; what happens to the child is going to depend essentially on the artist-therapist, who he is, and what he is. It is not a substitute for the multitude of decisions and interventions one has to deal with in child guidance problems. It provides us with a tool which not only facilitates therapy but also gives us a way of studying the healing and growth process itself. A physician may study a disease process by using a multitude of indicators daily to determine what is happening to the patient. He may use temperature, red-and-white blood-cell count, urinalysis, and a multitude of other variables. In studying the processes of the unconscious, we have a much harder time, and the use of the sandbox is an excellent way of observing and studying its workings.

This book represents a milestone in the emergence of a creative psychotherapy. Whether for the professional therapist or a generally interested person, this book promises to be an informative and involving work which cannot help but reach deeply into the reader's soul.

Like the fairy grandmother of our fairy tale, with her sandplay Mrs. Kalff has brought to us the refreshing fragrance of the mystery of life. In a time when science is supposed to solve all mysteries, she again makes life an eternal mystery, and the gift to each of us is an invisible ball of thread which we cannot see but can only feel; the core of that ball resides, for each of us, in that deep image-producing center of our being which so powerfully calls to us for help in its unfolding.

Harold Stone, Ph.D.
President
C. G. Jung Institute of
Los Angeles, California
1970

Chapter 1

SAND PLAY:
A Pathway to the Psyche

Working with children and adolescents, it has become clear to me that analogies occur which can be compared to the dynamics of the individuation process during childhood as they are described by Carl G. Jung. I would like to outline these findings with several case stories of development as they have happened in my playroom; first, however a few clarifications are necessary.

The results of my observations are in agreement with the psychological experience that the Self directs the psychic developmental process from the time of birth. The "Self," according to Jung, consists of "the sum of its conscious and unconscious, given facts (data)."[1] Man is born as a totality which, according to Eric Neumann is kept preserved for the time being within the mother's Self.[2] All the requirements of the newborn infant that make a direct appeal to the maternal instincts in general, such as appeasement of hunger, shelter from cold, etc. which are met by the bodily mother. We call this the phase of mother-child unity in which the child experiences an unconditional security and a sense of safety through motherly love.

After one year the Self of the child—that is to say, the center of his totality—separates itself from that of the mother. The child experiences security more and more in the *relationship* to the mother; in her caresses and displays of tenderness. A relationship of trust grows out of this experience.

The security which is the result of this first relationship is the basis of the third phase, which begins around the end of the sec-

[1] C. G. Jung, *Symbols of Transformation, Collected Works, Vol. 5 (New York: Pantheon Books, Inc., 1967).*
[2] *Erich Newumann, The Child* (New York: G. P. Putnam's Sons, 1973).

ond year of life and at the beginning of the third. During this phase, the center of the Self, is stabilized in the unconscious of the child and begins to manifest itself in symbols of wholeness.

Thus, the child plays, draws, paints or speaks in the ancient language of symbols with which adult man has, consciously or unconsciously, throughout the ages and in all cultures, expressed his wholeness. These symbols are either human figures of godly content, like the figures of Christ, Mary, Buddha, etc. or they are of a geometric or numerical nature, such as the circle or the square. We accept the validity of these symbols of the wholeness of the human psyche because they have occurred everywhere without exception from the earliest times of man. The circle, particularly as a "symbol of perfection and of the perfect being," is, as Jung puts it, "a well known expression of heaven, sun, God and for the ideal of man and the soul" [illustrations 1, 2, 3 and 4]. The square, my experience has shown, appears when wholeness is developing.

I have observed that in psychic development, the entity of

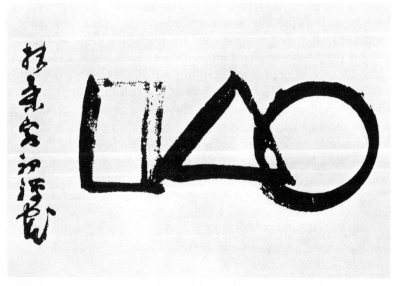

1   *Circle, triangle and square as original forms of the universe,* Sengai's The World of Zen.

2 Sand picture "Circle in Sand," done by 11-year-old boy.

3 Sun as image of God, Jung's Symbol of Transformation.

4 *Sand picture "Sun" of 15-year-old boy.*

5 *Painting of three-year-old boy (Collection of Rhoda Kellogg, San Francisco).*

6 *Chinese symbols for heaven (round) and earth (square), Chou-Dynasty.*
Chinese Art *by MacKenzie.*

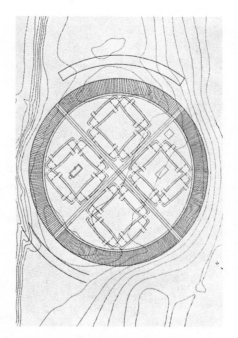

Excavation of a settlement of the Viking time, Denmark. Publication of the Danish National Museum.

four appears before the symbol of the circle or in connection with the circle [illustrations 5, 6 and 7].

My ideas were confirmed a few years ago in San Francisco when I saw Rhoda Kellogg's collection of children's artwork. During her many years as director of a nursery school, she collected thousands of drawings and finger paintings by children from two to four years of age. An enormous number of these pictures showed the familiar well-known symbols of wholeness.

Such symbols appear not only in drawings and paintings of children, but also in their verbal communication. A three-year-old boy asked me one day, "If it is true that the earth is round and that God can see everybody, does that mean He is like a circle?". Over each of his drawings, on the upper side of the picture, he drew a blue line from one end to the other. When I asked what the lines meant, he answered that it was God. These lines, each a very small part of an enormous circle, told of his conception.

Another boy of about the same age once discovered some tin

figures on my piano. He positioned them to form a full circle. He left the room for awhile, and when he came back, he brought a small, white porcelain dove and put it behind a photograph which was on the piano. When I asked him what the dove was doing in this hiding place, he answered, "We can't see God either."

Through such statements we can see the numinous content of the symbol. The circle is not only a geometrical form, it is also a symbol that brings to light something which lives invisibly in man. Symbols speak for the inner, energy-laden pictures, of the innate potentials of the human being which, when they are manifested, always influence the development of man. These symbols of a numinous or religious content tell of an inner drive for spiritual order which allow the relationship to the deity. This order gives man an inner security and insures for him, among other things, the development of his inherent personality.

I want to emphasize that *the manifestation of the Self, this inner order, this pattern for wholeness, is the most important moment in the development of the personality.* Psychotherapeutic work has proven, that a healthy development of the ego can take place only as a result of the successful manifestation of the Self, whether as a dream symbol or as a depiction in the sandbox. Such a manifestation of the Self seems to guarantee the development and consolidation of the personality.

On the other hand, in the case of a weak or neurotic ego development, I assume with certainty that this manifestation of the Self (through a symbol) has failed to appear. This may happen because the necessary motherly protection has not been given, or because the self-manifestation has been crucially disturbed by external influences such as war, illness, or lack of understanding from the environment in the child's earliest development. Therefore, I aim to give the child's Self the possibility of constellating and manifesting itself in therapy. And I try, through the transference, to protect it and to stabilize the relationship between the Self and the ego. This is possible within the psychotherapeutic relationship because it corresponds to the natural tendency of the psyche to constellate itself at the moment when a *free and sheltered space* is created.

This free space occurs in the therapeutic situation when the therapist is able to accept the child fully, so that he or she, as a person, is a part of everything going on in the room just as much as is the child himself. When a child feels that he is not alone—not only in his distress but also in his happiness—he then feels free but still protected, in all his expressions. Why is this relationship of confidence so important? Under certain circumstances, the situation of the first phase, the one of the mother-child unity, can be restored. This psychic situation can establish an inner peace which contains the potential for the development of the total personality, including its intellectual and spiritual aspects.

It is the role of the therapist to perceive these powers and, like the guardian of a precious treasure, protect them in their development. For the child, the therapist represents as a guardian, the space, the freedom and at the same time, the boundaries. The unique boundary of each development is meaningful because a transformation of psychic energy can occur only *within the boundaries of the individual.*

Gerhard Terstegen, a 17th-century mystic and pastor, lived by the following principle: "Whoever deals with souls must be like a nursemaid who leads the child by a halter and who only protects it from dangers and falls, but otherwise must leave the child to go its own way." It seems to me that he was saying that no unambiguous theories exist for the cure of souls, but that one should recognize the uniqueness of each person so that with the help of wise guidance, free development of the individuality can be guaranteed.

Development under the care of a therapist can be compared to the goal set by Pestalozzi in his work on education, *How Gertrud Teaches Her Children,* where he said that through genuine love by the mother, the child finds his way to inner unity and thus gains access to the divine.[3]

According to my experience, a healthy ego can only develop on the basis of the total security of the child; therefore I must assume that in case of a weak ego, the manifestation of the Self, as a symbol, which is normally observed at the ages of two to three years, had not taken place. Amazingly enough, I have

[3] J. H. Pestalozzi, *Wie Gertrud ihre Kinder lehrt,* Jung's Collected Works, Vol. 9 (Zurich: Racher, 1945).

found that where the symbolic manifestation of the Self was made possible during childhood, it can often be recovered to a certain degree in therapy. This recovery can occur at any stage of life.

Jung himself says:

In my experience it is of considerable practical importance that the symbols aiming at wholeness should be correctly understood by the doctor. They are the remedy with whose help neurotic dissociations can be repaired, by restoring to the conscious mind a spirit and an attitude which from time to time immemorial have been felt as solving and healing in their effects. They are représentations collectives *which facilitate the much-needed union of conscious and unconscious. This union cannot be accomplished either intellectually or in a purely practical sense, because in the former case the instincts rebel, and in the latter case, reason and morality. Every dissociation that falls within the category of the psychogenic neurosis is due to a conflict of this kind, and the conflict can only be resolved through the symbol.* [4]

In this sense, we can also understand Bachofen when he writes: "That is precisely the great dignity of the symbol, that it allows, and even stimulates, different degrees of comprehension, and leads from the truths of the physical life to those of a higher spiritual order."[5] The symbol embodies an image of a content transcending consciousness and points to the eternal foundation of our nature given us by God. Once recognized and experienced, it leads man to the actual dignity of his existence as a human being.

The symbol plays a great role in the sand play therapy, which I have expanded, based on the Lowenfeld's *World Technique.* [6] I use a sandbox with dimensions (57x72x7cm.)—that limits the player's imagination and thus acts as a regulating, protecting factor.

Hundreds of small figures of every conceivable type are provided. The child then arranges whichever figure he chooses on

[4] C. G. Jung, *Psychology and Religion*, "General Remarks on Symbolism," Collected Works, Vol. 11 (New York: Pantheon Books, Inc., 1963), p.191.

[5] J. J. Bachofen, *Mutterrecht and Urreligion* (Leipzig: Kroner, 1926).

[6] Ruth Bowyer, *Lowenfeld World Technique: Studies in Personality* (New York: Pergamon Press, Inc., 1970).

the sand. The sand picture which is produced by the child can be understood as a three-dimensional representation of some aspect of his psychic situation. An unconscious problem is played out in the sandbox, just like a drama; the conflict is transposed from the inner world to the outer world and made visible. This game of fantasy influences the dynamics of the unconscious in the child and thus affects his psyche.

The analyst interprets for himself the symbols emerging in the course of a series of sand pictures. The therapist's understanding of the problem which emerges in the picture often produces an atmosphere of trust between the analyst and the child, something like the original mother-child-unity, which exerts a healing influence. It is not necessary to communicate the therapist's insight to the child in words. We are dealing here with the previously mentioned *experience of the symbol in the free and sheltered space.* Under certain circumstances, however, the pictures are interpreted to the child in an easily understandable way that is connected with his life situation. With the help of the exterior picture, the inner problem is made visible and brings about the next step in development.

In addition, the details and composition of the pictures give the therapist an indication of the path to follow in the treatment. Frequently, the initial picture gives information about the situation and contains, hidden in the symbols, the goal to be aimed at: the realization of the Self. In this process, new energies which lead to the formation of a healthy ego development are freed.

An eight-year-old boy has represented the normal development of these energies very nicely in a sand picture [illustration 8]. In the upper right side of the picture the Self is embodied in the good shepherd with the sheep. Dark foreign powers (Moroccans) in orderly rows move toward the space which can be regarded as representing the boy's inner peace. The powers are armed. The boy remarked, however, "Actually they wouldn't need to be armed," sensing he could cope with them.

My experience coincides with Erich Neumann's theory of the stages of ego-development[7]. These are: 1) the animal, vegetative stage; 2) the fighting stage; and 3) the adaptation to the collec-

---

7 Erich Neumann, *The Child* (New York: G. P. Putnam's Sons, 1973).

tive. In the first phase, the ego expresses itself chiefly in pictures which animals and vegetation predominate. The next stage brings battles, which appear again and again, especially in puberty. By now, the child is so strengthened that he can take upon himself the battle with external influences and he can come to grips with them. Finally, he is admitted to the environment as a person and becomes a member of the collective.

While studying Chinese thought, I came across a diagram which, it seems to me, corresponds to our viewpoint [illustration 9]. It is the diagram of Chou-Tun-Yi, a philosopher of the Sung period, who lived around the year 1000 AD. The beginning of all things is shown in a circle, in which I see an analogy to the Self at birth. A second circle shows the interfusing action of yin and yang which produces the five elements. I am inclined to relate this circle to what I have said about the manifestation of the Self. It contains the germ of those energies which lead to the formation of the ego and the development of personality [illustrations 10 and 11]. Just as the five elements arise from this constellation, the personality develops around the centering point of the ego. I equate this step with development in the first half of life. Also, in our tradition, five is also the number of the natural man [illustrations 12 and 13]. Here, man is seen as a pentagram with his head and outstretched arms and legs—a microcosm in the macrocosm.

The third circle could be compared with the manifestation of

Diagram of the Supreme Ultimate

The Ultimateless!
Yet also the Supreme Ultimate!

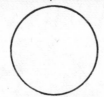

Yang
Movement

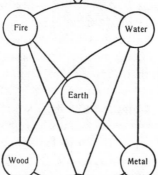

Yin
Quiescence

Fire

Water

Earth

Wood

Metal

The *Ch'ien* Principle
becomes the male
element

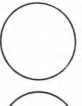

The *K'un* Principle
becomes the female
element

Production and Evolution of
All Things

9

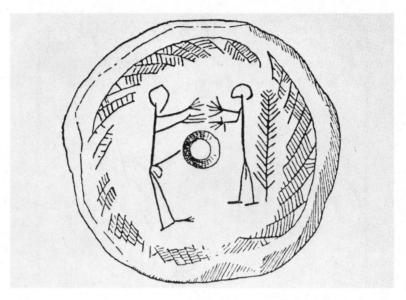

10

11

12

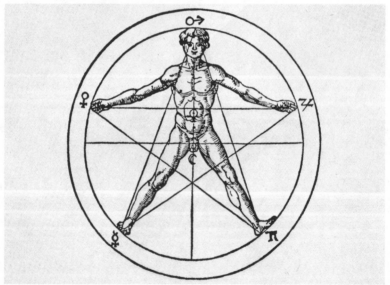

13

the Self in the individuation process during the second half of life. In the fourth circle, I see the ending as opposed to the beginning: the end of the movement which leads from life to death. Following the law of transformation, on which the diagram is based, death—just like the sacrifice of a psychic situation lived to its conclusion—holds the germ of new life.

14

These images may show us that in all traditions, our lives correspond to a physical and psychic flow which can be looked on as the basis of individual development. Therefore, it seems to me that our therapeutic efforts with the child and adolescent will do justice only as seen from this view.

The children who come to me for treatment suffer mostly from lack of inner security; they have no feeling of belonging. Something prevents the normal growth which is necessary for their inner balance—it may be an unfavorable home or outside-the-home situation. Because of this, I believe that it is very important not to separate the place of my practice from the environment and atmosphere of my home where it occurs. When my heavy entrance door closes (my house was first constructed in 1485)—[illustration 14], the child enters an old, paneled room in which a magnificent tile stove is quite prominent. It is easy to climb a few built-in steps leading to the top of the stove. The child can now do what he feels like doing. He is allowed to sit or lie on the stove, to look down on the room or out through the window, where he can watch the birds which play and bathe in the little fountain in my garden. He can look at some picture books or read magazines. He may also feel encouraged to investigate the unusual objects and pictures in my old house. Its irregular order of rooms and staircases heightens its interest; small children often love to play hide-and-seek, while the older ones sometimes become adventurous and look for hidden treasures. If possible, I give them free range of the house. Often I take them to the basement, where they investigate the metre-thick walls to see if there are subterranean passages, or we go to the immense attic with its secret double floors which invite them to explorations. The children are always looking for something hidden; a treasure which they would like to find in themselves—which they have been unable to discover so far.

My house was constructed hundreds of years ago on rock; its rooms were not built and shaped with yardstick and compass, but grew according to a natural law. This house offers an atmosphere which corresponds to the natural temperament of young people. Even more, the child comes upon a world which is completely open to him, and where he *is totally welcomed and accepted.* As he enters the playroom where the sandtray is waiting, the chain of tension , which perhaps arose by wondering: "What will I find, what will I have to do?", is broken.

There are many things in my playroom: paints, clay, mosaic, plaster of Paris, etc. lay invitingly open on a large table. The sandtrays are close by and on a shelf are hundreds of little figures made of lead and other materials: people—not only of various types and professions of modern times, but also figures from past centuries, Negroes, fighting Indians, etc. There are also wild and domestic animals, houses of different styles, trees, bushes, flowers, fences, traffic signals, cars, trains, old carriages, boats; in short, everything which exists in the world as well as in fantasy.

All of the items listed above are the material which Dr.

Lowenfeld has collected for her *World Play*[8]. She understood to place herself in the world of the child; with ingenious intuition, she created a game which enables the child to build a world—*his* world—in a sandbox [illustrations 15a, 15b]. The size of the box corresponds exactly to what the eye can encompass. From among the numerous objects, the child chooses those which particularly appeal to him and which are meaningful. He forms hills, tunnels, plains, lakes and rivers in the sand, just as he views the world from his own situation, and he allows the figures to act as he experiences them in his fantasy.

The child has absolute freedom in determining what to construct, which figures to choose and how to use them. The same limitations that are prerequisite for genuine freedom in the real world, are present in the measurements of the sandbox, which are scaled down to man's size, thereby setting up limits as to what can be represented and providing a frame wherein the transformation can take place. The child experiences, quite unconsciously, what I call a *free*, and at the same time, a *protected space*. Using several cases I try to illustrate the experience which occurs within this space. I am aware, however, that in order to protect the patients, I had to omit certain information.

[8] Margaret Lowenfeld, *The Non-Verbal Thinking of Children and Its Place in Psychology* (London: The Institute of Child Psychology, 1964).

15a

15b

Chapter 2

CHRISTOPH:
Overcoming of an Anxiety Neurosis

Nine-year-old Christoph had come to my house led by his father, a tall farmer. The boy gave the impression of being overly delicate and anxious, but at my request, he willingly followed me into the playroom. Hesitating, yet curious, he looked around. Small curls framed his pale forehead. Was this supposed to be a child from the countryside? After a while his glance fell on the small, cap pistol which lay at some distance from him. "would you like to play with it?" I asked him. A slight, but definite, defensive movement told me that he was afraid of the pistol.

I learned from his father that the school authorities had requested that the boy see a psychologist because he frequently played truant. Each day, Christoph left his house punctually for school and returned home at the expected time. His mother therefore had had no idea that there were many times when he had not gone to school. Christoph lived with his parents and a brother, who was two years younger, in fairly isolated, rural surroundings. On his way to the village school, he passed through meadows with fruit trees. What he might have done while the other children were in school, no one knew.

He glanced at the sandtray. "Have you ever played with sand?" I asked.

"Yes, I used to," he answered, "but now that's only for my little brother. I'm too big for that."

"But I bet you haven't played in sand with toys and figures like these." I showed him my collection.

That appealed to him and he quickly set to work. In the middle of the sandtray appeared a large hill; with great care, he hollowed out a tunnel. He was satisfied only when he could see straight through it. Then he turned to the figures. A small house seemed to please him, and he placed it in the lower left corner. Next to it he put a swing. He fenced these in without making any opening for entering or leaving. On the top of the hill he planted a tall poplar tree, under its shelter, beneath it, he positioned a small child on a bench. A narrow path led from the mound to the plain below [illustration 16].

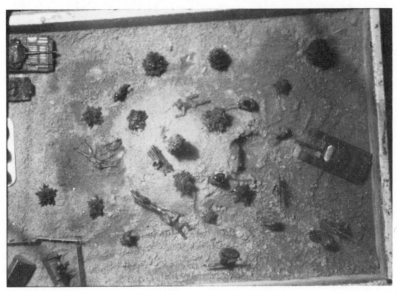

16

Suddenly he became lively and selected heavy tanks, soldiers and weapons, which he placed around and all over the hill. A war had broken out, he said. Soldiers besieged the hill, machine gunners shot through the tunnel, and the tanks were prepared for combat. He even wanted a bomber plane to be hung from the ceiling by a thread so that the hill could also be attacked from the air. The boy who had been so shy and worried at the beginning of the hour, now seemed to be gripped by a passion until everything was exactly the way he wanted. Then Christoph looked at his picture with satisfaction and made sure that the bomber would not miss its target. Before leaving the room, he suddenly put a filling station on the left edge of the picture. His face was aglow as he went to meet his father, whom he asked to look at what he had done.

On the one hand, the picture showed a peaceful situation, the way it might be at his home: a house, a small garden, and a small boy on a swing. Here, he seemed to feel at ease. At the same time, up on the hill near a tall poplar tree, there sat another boy with whom Christoph identified himself as well.

A tree, rooted deeply in the nourishing earth, its trunk growing up towards the sky and its branches unfolding into a crown—that blooms in spring and carries fruit in autumn—has preoccupied man from time immemorial. Its growth is compared with man's life; in many cultures, it is represented as the tree of life. In its shade, men seek protection, and its fruit appeases hunger and quenches thirst. In this way, it embodies the protecting and nourishing elements.

The boy was dreaming up there on the hilltop, longing to develop his talents in the shelter of the tree, which would allow him to take his proper place in the world. But then, on the other hand, the war raged around the hill, threatening this wish. The outside world seemed to him an unconquerable opponent, and anxiously he withdrew into his *Temenos:* the fenced-in, sheltered space of his house.

As I looked at his hill, I was reminded involuntarily of the shape of a pregnant woman's abdomen, and I wondered why, of all things, this hill would be the target of those attacks. Could it be that the mother had gone through an unfortunate pregnancy? Was the boy searching for feminine protection other than from his own mother, which drove him to the situation under the tree on the hill? I concluded that a discussion with Christoph's mother might provide some information.

She told me that as the daughter of a farmer, she had had a difficult life. Often she did not feel well and suffered from abdominal pains; however, little attention was paid to this. Instead, she was scolded for being lazy when she felt ill. The pains continued even after she married. She was afraid of becoming pregnant, and she needed reassurance from several doctors that there was nothing to worry about in giving birth to a child. As soon as she became pregnant, the fear of the delivery became almost unbearable. Again, she needed the constant reassurance of a doctor. Finally, she was able to wait patiently for the birth.

She had a normal delivery. However, she had hardly begun to take on the responsibility for the infant, when she was plagued with new fears.

We might assume, therefore, the boy never really found a feeling of security with his mother. It is even possible to conceive that the fears of the mother were transferred to the child.

Besides this, little Christoph had experienced a great many unfortunate episodes in his younger life. When he was barely two years old, he stuck his finger in a wall socket and received an electric shock. Before he had begun school, he was operated on for a hernia, which also seemed to have intimidated him constantly. His mother told me that he was very frightened of injections and doctors in white coats. He was afraid of the dark, and at night he feared going upstairs alone in his room.

During his second year in school, he had a teacher who handled the children roughly. This increased his anxiety and may have led eventually to his staying away from school from time to time. At this point, he also began to steal small objects from his mother, especially candy.

As a first step it became necessary to give the boy the security to enable him to face the difficulties in life.

In his picture, he had shown that he was looking for a safe place outside his home: he saw himself on top of the hill being sheltered by the tree, for he was seeking a symbolic mother. On the other hand, the tree is also a symbol of the Self. It embodies not only maternal femininity, but its straight trunk also has a phallic meaning. Thus, it is a carrier of the union of opposites. From a prognostic point of view, I could hope that a centering of the natural energies within the boy would be possible. I was also pleased that Christoph put a filling station at the left edge of the picture at the last minute. New energies could spring from the unconscious!

By the second session, he seemed to be completely at ease with me. He would decide which game to play. At first, a small store was the greatest attraction. He wanted to come to it and buy things from me. There were fruits of all kinds, groceries and candy. He bought large quantities of oranges. No wonder, since the shining sphere contained a sweet, juicy fruit and seeds that symbolized new life, which was what the boy's unconscious was striving to attain.

One day, the peaceful game came to an abrupt end. Suddenly, Christoph staged a raid on the store. Christoph was the attacker and I was made the policeman who had to look for him. Christoph had great fun hiding in the secret places of our old house, and I had to search for him a long time. Often, I prolonged the search on purpose to show him how well he had hidden himself. Wasn't this game showing how Christoph wanted me to uncover his own inner secrets? He wanted to be taken seriously; he wanted to be searched for.

One day he revealed that he, just like his father, was fond of drawing. He wanted to draw on the large, white board (2.50x1m). But I was surprised when, in spite of his wish to be permitted to use the large surface, he painted a tiny man in the bottom corner. Yes, that was still the size of his small ego!

After a month he made a second sand picture. Again, a boy sat on a hill with a small village spread out below. Ducks and geese walked about on the village square. Suddenly he changed the peaceful village into a battleground by placing fighting soldiers throughout the entire village. Cars and a train were left stuck in the hill. This picture demonstrated that hardly any progress had been achieved in the preceding month.

Nevertheless, Christoph became bolder and bolder. He even became interested in the cap pistol. He wanted to know what could be done with it. First I showed him how to hold it so that the trigger could be squeezed. Finally, he also wanted to hear the noise. He wanted me to shoot and he would stand far away and put his fingers in his ears. Two or three times, he watched and listened, then he wanted to make it work himself. He wanted it louder and louder. At last, we ended up in the cellar, where he exploded countless detonator caps on the stone floor. I could not supply him with enough caps, and the louder the noise, the happier he became.

About four months went by before he made another sand picture. With his hands, he drew broad streets in the sand with some cars moving about. In contrast to his first pictures, this one appeared empty and meaningless; however, it was the first time that no obstacles were placed in the road. The cars could circulate freely: the damned-up libido was beginning to flow! I hope that it would not take long for a definite step forward to be seen in his life.

In the next hour, he again drew on the large white board. This time, he filled almost all the available space. The picture represented a ski race. Many people lined the ski track to watch a skier who was dashing downhill.

This picture confirmed my impression that the energy held back in his unconscious was being acted, in motion and was now trying to move toward a goal. The outer world, where at first the fighting soldiers had represented the obstacles to his development, had now changed into the crowd that was watching and admiring the achiever (the skier). It was very clear to me that there lay hidden considerable ambition in this seemingly delicate child.

It was too soon to assume that Christoph was already capable of handling this energy, but I was delighted to perceive that the healing influence of the psyche had begun to come through. The drawing hinted at the child's potential; however, the weak strokes indicated to me that the next step was clearly defined. Its realization however, still lay in the future. From my past observations, I know that at least six to eight weeks are needed before a situation that is just becoming visible as it emerges from the unconscious, can push through into the outer life. It is as delicate as a newly-sprouting blade of grass that needs attentive care.

With increased confidence, I looked forward to Christoph's next session.

He came a week later, but the expression on his face worried me. He was paler than ever and he looked around anxiously. What could have happened? I greeted him with the question, "How are you?"

"Not well," he answered. "I've just seen an accident."

Christoph had to take a short train ride to come to see me. He had seen a postman, who was bringing packages to the train, fall from his wagon as the train began to move. The man was not hurt at all; however, the few seconds of uncertainty before Christoph knew whether the postman was badly hurt or not were enough to destroy the security that was just beginning to build within him.

This was all very clearly expressed in the sand picture that he made while still suffering from the effects of the accident [illustration 17]. He put the figures in the sand totally at random.

Tanks, soldiers, domesticated animals, as well as those from the steppes and the jungle, filled the sandbox to the rim without any grouping or design. A train was stuck in the sand. The representation reminded me of pictures of schizophrenics. In my concern over this big setback that the boy had suffered, I tried to look for some positive elements: on the lower left side was a small pond. In front near a large blossoming tree, sat a small boy and a woman with their backs to the chaos. An elephant was the only animal turning towards the pond to drink water.

Christoph added, "I wouldn't like to live in a world like that." He was seeking refuge in the therapeutic situation he had represented by the child and woman. He had already experienced that security could be found here, and he knew that he gained new strength from unknown sources (his own unconscious, symbolized by the water). Here, too, the tree in bloom represented the Self, which directs the growth process. The elephant, which could be seen as belonging to the group, probably stood for the high demands the boy carried in himself.

Animals represent various aspects of human instincts, but at the same time also their significance. The elephant possesses a high degree of intelligence and helps man with his work in the jungle. In India, it is holy because it is the legendary creator of Buddha. Therefore it embodies, among other things, the preconscious animal form of the Redeemer.

By saying that he did not want to live in that kind of world, Christoph had given expression to his hope for redemption, which he unconsciously and symbolically revealed in the small group around the pond. Of course, the overwhelming force of the chaotic situation that surrounded him still seemed much too powerful.

At that point in time, Christoph's teacher had established contact with me, and I was gratified to learn from him that the boy was no longer skipping school. However, he was having great difficulty in keeping up with his classmates in his studies. The teacher therefore suggested that Christoph be transferred to a special class. I was afraid that this might cause a new shock for the boy. His ambition, which slumbered in his unconscious but showed up so strongly in his pictures, would at least be hurt;

the little security that Christoph had gained might be destroyed again.

I asked the teacher to be patient and, if at all possible, to keep Christoph in the class. It seemed crucial at this time to give Christoph every opportunity to become psychically stronger. It was important at this critical point to save and to further develop the gains which had been so hard to achieve and which had already threatened to disappear.

In therapy, more ways had to be found which could restore Christoph's shaky trust in himself.

When he came for the next hour, he discovered a broken-down electric locomotive. He wanted to take it apart, find out why it wouldn't work, and repair it. Even older boys had tried to do the same without success, nevertheless, I let him do as he pleased. He took great pains loosening the small screws and tiny parts and laid them in precise order on the table in front of him. I admired his manual dexterity and the care with which he handled even the tiniest pieces. By the end of the hour, they all lay neatly in rows. Would it be possible for Christoph to put them back together in the right order? He asked me to leave the parts just as he had placed them.

In the two succeeding hours, Christoph sat at the table, intensely occupied with reconstructing the small locomotive. From time to time, he tried it out; when it would not function, he would again change something. Suddenly it began to move. What a surprise! What joy! He quickly constructed a train track on the floor.

After that, many hours passed with both of us on the floor, while he instructed me about throwing switches and stopping trains. Because I am not very good in these matters, anyway, I let him direct me. He obviously enjoyed this, and if I forgot something, such as throwing a switch, it would give him the chance to correct me. He became my teacher in this game and thus grew into a new role. Here, *he* knew something which *I* still had to learn!

After five weeks of intense playing, I suggested a sand picture, and Christoph quickly agreed [illustration 18]. A wide bridge leading out of a forest spanned a river on which boats were cruising in both directions. On the bridge itself was heavy traffic. A train and some cars were rushing back and forth.

17

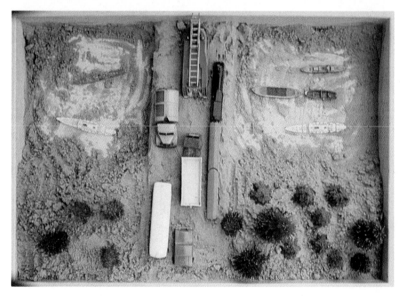

18

Many forces and new energies had been set in motion and were emerging from the unconscious, represented by the forest. By looking more closely, I noticed that some of the vehicles had definite regulating functions: for instance, the fire engine rushed to put out the flames and the garbage truck collected the trash. Regulatory energies which resolved the chaotic condition of the preceding picture were now moving. The traffic circulated in both directions, on the water as well as on land. This indicated that the powers were fully freed, yet in orderly flow, and were establishing the interconnection between the unconscious and conscious. At this time, I realized that a healthy psychic development was underway.

It seeemed to me that the boy was a born electrician; he repaired the train, handled it with great skill, and enriched it with all kinds of electrical details. In order to make it easier for him to stay home alone upstairs with his brother, I suggested that Christoph install a small Morse-code set which could operate from one floor to another. Sending signals back and forth created fun for both children and parents.

While he was with me, I gave him the task of installing electric lights in my three-story dollhouse. Because a house is a symbol for man's inner being, I wanted him symbolically to light up his inner environment (*Lebensraum*). Christoph was again thrilled with his work. With great concentration, he threaded the delicate wires and mounted the tiny lights and switches. After several hours' work, all the lights in six rooms could be turned on and off. The amazement over Edison's invention of the electric light bulb in the last century could hardly have been greater than the effect on Christoph when all the rooms of the dollhouse could be lit up at once. And on top of that, it was his own work!

This gave rise to a further sand picture [illustration 19]. A musician sat playing a harmonica on a small hill in the center. Around the hill, circus figures moved clockwise and counter clockwise within a closed circle. Roman chariots, elephants, tigers, and horses, as well as clowns and an acrobat, were elements of the circus. The spectators were placed outside, to the left and right. The Self, which was revealed in the preceding picture in the form of a square by the water, the bridge and the means of transportation moving in all four directions, had now

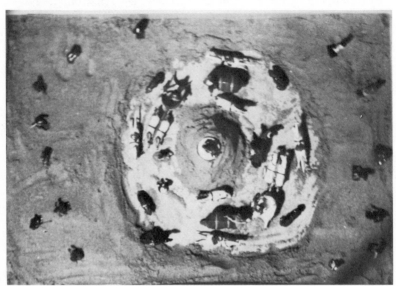

19

20

clearly and significantly developed into a circumambulation around a center.

To clarify my strong emotion about this event I would like to go into the symbolism of the circumambulation. In Latin, "Circus" means "ring" or "circle." In ancient Rome, the circus served principally for the Roman chariot races, and later for animal fights. During the Christian persecution, the Christians were sentenced to fight the animals in the arena.

Was it possible that the nine-year-old boy had already heard of the Roman chariot races? Certainly not. Living far from town in simple surroundings, he had never had the opportunity to go to the circus, although he might have heard about it. It was more likely that he had heard of trained animals like elephants and tigers, which circled around in the picture with the horses. Because it is not common to have Roman chariots in circuses today, we were confronted here with an archetype.

The musician in the middle, Christoph explained, made music for everyone to enjoy. In this picture it is clearly a question of a concentration towards the middle. On closer examination, I could see that the two outer circles moved from right to left (counterclockwise), which is psychologically comparable to a movement towards the unconscious, while the inside figures described a circle from left to right (clockwise), psychologically in the direction towards consciousness.

We know that a centering in man is equivalent to a numinous experience; i.e., coming in contact with man's inherent religious forces. Thus it would not be too farfetched to make an anology with the three circular movements of the priest with the censer (twice from right to left and once from left to right) over the offering at a Catholic mass. The offering is blessed and prepared for the actual transformation. The boy's picture surely represented a centering process signifying a transformation. Here, in an apparently unimportant game, was expressed in a deeply moving way the archetypal function of the healing psyche. Was it actually possible that the negative forces, represented in the picture by the Roman chariots and fighting animals, were about to be transformed through a still unconscious, but deeply religious, event?

The circle itself, and the circling around the central point in particular, has a godly character in other cultures as well. Jung mentions this in *Psychology and Religion:*

> *Since olden times the circle with a center has been a symbol for the Deity, illustrating the wholeness of God incarnate: the single point in the center and the series of points constituting the circumference.*

And further on:

> *Psychologically, this arrangement is equivalent to a mandala and is thus a symbol of the Self, the point of reference not only of the individual ego, but of all those who are of like mind or who are bound together by fate. The Self is not ego, but a supraordinate totality embracing the conscious and the unconscious. But since the latter has no assignable limits and in its deep layers is of a collective nature, it cannot be distinguished from that of another individual. As a result, it continually creates that ubiquitous participation mystique which is the unity of many, the* one *in all men*[9].

To protect himself from disintegration, as might be feared from the representation in illustration 17, the boy had succeeded in creating a *temenos* in his innermost being, by way of a transference situation that brought about a mother-child unity. From this protected space, it would now be possible for him to cope with the outer world. If we recall the first picture, the inside and outside were not in harmony. In the protection of his home he was fine; up on the hill he felt terribly threatened. In his latest sand picture, he had symbolically expressed the centering that normally takes place in two- or three-year-old children. From this point, a strong and healthy ego should develop.

He became interested in painting and clay modeling, showing further skills with his hands and revealing a very good sense of color. During this phase, I gave the child increasing opportunities to be active in a creative way. It is not a matter of creating perfect works of art, but of investigating ideas and trying to express them.

The developmental level of the infant that Neumann mentions has to be reestablished during therapy.[10] Also at a later

---

9 C. G. Jung, *Psychology and Religion: East and West,* Collected Works, Vol. 11 (New York: Pantheon Books, Inc., 1963), p. 276.

10 Erich Neumann, *The Child* (New York: G. P. Putnam's Sons, 1973).

21

22

/ 57

stage, this first phase manifests itself on the vegetative, animalistic level. Images often are produced with representations of vegetation and of animals. It was like this with Christoph, too. The next picture portrayed a jungle [illustration 20]. A river with natural banks connected by a ford and a bridge flowed through the middle of a wooded region. Animals moved towards the stream for a drink. On the extreme right on each side of the water stood a Morrocan. In these two dark-skinned people I saw the ego as it was beginning to delineate itself from and instinctive level, dwelling deep in the unconscious—and represented here by the jungle.

In daily life, Christoph was showing himself increasingly self-reliant; his ambition began to assert itself more and more. Good marks became important. I was invited to assist at an examination in order to see his progress for myself.

It wasn't long before this new tackling of his environment was expressed in a picture [illustration 21]. Whereas the water in the former picture was flowing between natural banks, this time it was channeled into a man-made canal. Ships moved in both directions. On both sides, soldiers were fighting and dark-skinned men were battling over the Suez Canal, as Christoph told me. In place of the darker trees, which recalled the jungle, there were palms which grow in the Near East and Southern Europe. Elephants were also present.

Let us imagine a jungle scene, such as we might find in Africa. If we look psychologically, we would witness a scene on a deeper unconscious level than one taking place in the Near East by a man-made canal. Therefore, one might assume the ego development in the boy was emerging more forcefully. Moreover, the fight raged around a canal, built by man, as a scientific project. Therefore, it was obviously important to encourage the boy in every way in this context to do something that could also be useful to him in a profession later on in life. Among other things, he built a small, funicular railway on his own initiative, linking his friend's house to his own. However, all the plans were discussed with me, and I offered him help in completing it. The funicular also represented a link with the outer world, which he needed very much for his future.

The school, which had caused so much worry in the beginning, was now hardly any problem. He worked with perseverance in the subjects that gave him the most trouble. The threat of being transferred to a special class had long passed. Even if he wasn't a brilliant pupil, he was certainly prepared for future professional or vocational training.

The last picture [illustration 22] that he made during therapy showed the hill that separates the Lake of Zurich from Lake Greifen. A few houses represented the villages, and the men near them were the inhabitants. A street wound around the hill. At the high point—at the top of the pass, as it were—sat a boy. He sat in complete freedom on the hill, in the region where his home is. This showed that the adjustment to the world was finally accomplished. The picture represents the transformation of those forces which, in the initial picture, were expressed by aggression and which hindered the child's development. Where fighting soldiers had formerly besieged the hill and had threatened the boy on his bench under the poplar tree, there now stood men who could pursue their work in peace. The boy, who had seen himself in the first picture in a narrowly limited home situation, surrounded by the din of war, was now waiting on the hill, near the edge of the street for the bus that he said would take him out into the world.

Chapter 3

KIM:
Cure of an
Inhibition to Learn

Twelve-year-old Kim did not know how to enjoy his life. His father described him as lonely, without friends, withdrawn and often bored. Games had not interested him since his earliest childhood. Now and then, he read a book, but without any great interest. In the company of adults he appeared very well-adjusted. His clothing was always correct and his hair neatly combed; although he gave an impression of neatness, Kim worried his father. The boy's first school years passed without any great difficulties, yet his withdrawal from comrades of his own age became more and more obvious. Sometimes his learning abilities seem to be impaired; he was tested for intelligence, however, and was found to have a good average. He started therapy, but without notable success. The advice of the therapist was to send him to a boarding school, where it was hoped it would be easier for him to find friends of his own age with whom he could participate in sports and games. But his father did not want to be separated from his son. Since his wife's death several years earlier, he had clung tightly to Kim.

And here begins Kim's story. At the tender age of two, he lost his mother. A nurse undertook to bring him up, as well as a brother, who was about a year younger. For six years, she played the role of mother to the boys and was loved by both. It was the father who appeared to suffer most from the loss of his wife. Time failed to heal his wounds; on the contrary, the pain grew worse. He left the place where he had established his family and his work. Even more serious was the fact that he could not decide on a new field of work. A constant unrest had taken possession of him, and unrest means insecurity. How could he, in his condition, give the little boys the necessary security?

Thus, after the younger son had been sent to a boarding school on the advice of a therapist, Kim's father wanted to preserve what was left of the family relationship by being together with his older son. This was a human, absolutely understandable wish that, in my judgment, should be taken into consideration, if it were at all possible.

According to his intelligence and ability, 12-year-old Kim was assigned to the first year of junior high school (college preparatory school). He was not an outstanding pupil; Latin seemed to be most difficult for him. The question the troubled father raised with me was: Will my son be capable of going through the junior high school without separating him from me?

It would be expecting too much from a therapist to answer a question like that with "yes" or "no." Nothing is more complex, more delicate and exposed to a variety of influences than the psyche. But the development of its forces comes when a free, and yet protected, space is established. Only then will the psyche's possibilities become visible, which we often view as a miracle. The psyche has an inherent tendency to heal itself; the task is given to the therapist to prepare the path for this tendency. But it would be pure boasting to assert, on the basis of the inherent healing tendency, that the path will be found in every case. Nevertheless, as long as there seems to be the possibility of healing, every case is worth an earnest try.

When Kim entered my therapy room for the first time, I got the impression of a boy who was not really young. I felt that what mattered in his life was buried deep within himself.

He greeted me very politely yet somewhat inquisitively. Nothing seemed to disturb his correct attitude (behavior). I was convinced he would not play for the time being. I would not even dare to ask him to do so, for this would have made him even more unapproachable and probably would have injured his dignity.

We talked of school and Latin, but after awhile, he began to yawn. That was the best expression for his complete lack of interest. For this reason, I knew that private tutoring would not help, nor would a change of milieu bring about any substantial improvement of the situation. This listlessness was the expression of a one-sided development, for which the cause still had to be found.

When he came to the second session, he acted much livelier. He asked me right away if he could build a barricade in my sandbox. Astonished by his own suggestion to play, I showed him the figures he could use. Something that had seemed to be impossible was about to be realized. The sand was first carefully mixed with water so that it could be easily formed [illustration 23]. Then, with an unbelievable devotion, walls were built up which actually represented a whole system of barricades. Heavy weapons such as tanks, cannons and bombers were, as it seemed, put in for defense by exact calculation. The left side of the sandbox at first remained empty. Only after he was content with the completion of the right side—after he had again and again convinced himself that the weapons could not be seen from the other side—did he turn to the left one. There, three light-artillery units were placed, comparatively quickly, behind a moderately weak tin shelter. he looked at the whole thing; almost unnoticeably, he finally added an airplane, which he defined as having crashed in the carefully built-up defense system.

23

The inequality of the opposed fields of force gave rise in me to the only question which I posed to the boy during the whole hour: "Can these three weak artillery units really withstand the heavy weapons?" His answer was: "One never knows."

These words moved me deeply, for, unconsciously, he had expressed in his answer the possiblity of a healing.

The crashed airplane showed his own situation. His whole life was, until now, directed towards the conscious. He was intelligent, he could learn, he had acquired social manners, and he could accommodate himself to everything imposed from outside. However, something in him was almost smothered. It was the creativity in him, that which really constitutes the essence of man.

In the beginning developmental phase of puberty, when the boy develops into a man and the girl into a woman, it is of extreme importance that access to the inherent energy sources which guarantee the development of the personality be intact. In his case, it had been endangered since his early youth. The child, born out of the protecting enclosure of the mother's womb into the world, still requires the protection of the mother for a long time. Through the care and, above all things, through the love the mother gives the child, she implants a feeling of security, *the* only security which is necessary for the child to develop according to his own potential. If the mother is lost, the child will retreat inside himself. To protect himself against influences from the environment, he erects a bulwark around his innermost being. Behind such a rampart, fear is hidden which, when it becomes too great, changes into aggression. If the aggression is repressed—if it cannot manifest itself—it consumes so much inner energy that little remains for anything new in life. Thus, the child suddenly refuses to function when "too much" is expected of him. In this case, the demand that Kim begin the study of Latin became "too much." It is easily understandable that a sensitive child, frightened by a demand which seems too great, will lose courage and show a lack of interest in what is demanded of him. This poses problems for parents and teachers alike.

The crashed airplane in the sandtray picture was an expression of what he felt to be his hopeless situation. It lay in that area where the repressed aggression was represented in the form of heavy weapons behind sheltering walls. This was the situation in which he lived until the moment of his first sandtray picture. This was actually the first creative game that began to animate his stiffened attitude. The dynamics blocked in him were represented in the three light-artillery units behind the moderately weak structure. That there were three seemed meaningful to me, inasmuch as three is a dynamic number. Wherever we meet it, it is always connected with some course of events having a beginning and a goal. In fairy tales, for example, we know of the three difficult tasks that the young man must carry out in order to conquer his princess and finally win the kingdom.

Our boy had to reach his kingdom too, which consisted in becoming, as an individual according to his abilities, a useful member of the collective. Is not everyone his own master and king who is enabled with his talents and gifts to carry out a task which daily revives him and makes him happy? It does not matter in what field—whether he works as a craftsman or in the intellectual discipline. But what would the king be without his kingdom? And above all, from where does he take the almost more-than-human power to lead and rule it?

In a further symbolic meaning, the number three holds a clue as to how this power is to be reached. Since ancient times, not only is the number three regarded as a dynamic force, but it is also defined as holy. Thousands of years before Christianity, acts of divine nature were connected with it.

Thus, the three seems to be connected with a super human power. Jung says of this, in his psychological interpretation of *The Dogma of Trinity*: "The Trinity is an archetype whose dominating energies not only fosters spiritual development, but may on occasion, actually enforce it."[11] Under the protection of these divine energies, which were known in the unconscious of our boy, the hope arose of victory over his overwhelming aggressions by his apparently still-weak energies which essentially "are bigger than our ego."

It lies in the hands of the therapist to intercept such powers as they become manifest in a child and to protect them in order to give them the possibility of becoming effective.

---

[11] C. G. Jung, *Experimental Researches,* Collected Works, Vol. 2 (New York: Pantheon Books, Inc., 1973), p.2.

I am deeply moved again and again at the discovery of how close the child's psyche is to spiritual and healing forces. The simple words of the child, "one never knows," expressed at the same time a profound, worldly wisdom which reminded me of the Chinese sage, LAO-TSE. We find in Chapter 76 of the *Tao Teh Ching* something valid for men in the West as well as the East:

> *Man, when he enters into life,*
> *is tender and weak,*
> *And when he dies,*
> *then he is tough and strong.*
>
> *That is why the tough and the strong are*
> *companions of death,*
> *the tender and the weak,*
> *companions of life.*
>
> *For this reason:*
> *If the weapons are strong, we will not be victorious.*

and in Chapter 78:

> *That which is weak conquers that which is strong,*
> *and what is tender conquer what is tough,*
> *To everyone on the earth this is known,*
> *but no one wants to act by this.*[12]

Lao-tse expresses the possibility of the weak triumphing over the strong, which to this day has been proven again and again throughout history, where the weak gained unsuspected powers, thanks to their deep faith. This often led to their victory.

When Kim came to the next session, he wanted to build a bulwark again [illustration 24]. Delighted at his desire to play and in excited expectation of how his condition would develop, I gladly let him do as he pleased. A further barricade was made, but in a somewhat looser form. When he looked at it, he said, "This is not built up as much as before." As a matter of fact, the walls were not so high anymore, and it seemed as if the boy had already started to remove the protective walls.

In the following hour, Kim went without delay to the sandbox [illustration 25]. Walls were again built, but this time it was

12 Lao-tse, *Tao-te-king, Das Buch von Sinn und Leben,* translated and annotated by Richard Wilhelm, Eugen Diederichs (Dusseldorf/Koln, 1957).

24

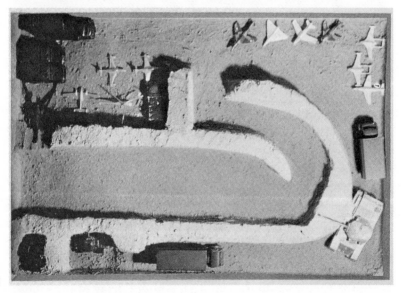

25

a runway behind which the airplanes and bombers were waiting ready for take-off. The runway was big and wide, directed towards the left, the side of the still-unexperienced possibilities. This meant that the way was opened for his unusually intense aggressions, which had been blocked off before.

How would this happen in a boy who had never in all his life, consciously destroyed anything? I awaited the answer in excitement.

At the next sitting, he no longer wanted to play in the sand. When I asked him what he wanted to do, he looked around and discovered some darts, which he threw at the target meant for them. However, after a short time it bored him to use the target, and he began to throw the darts at my freshly-painted paneled wall. So much energy was put into his throwing that the splinters fell from the wooden walls. Probably to his great amazement, I let him do as he liked, and for the first time, his features lit up. That I didn't blame him nor express myself, as for example: "It is terrible, how you demolish my room!" gave him the feeling that there was something here which would help him.

The game with the darts was not enough, though. A small air gun seemed more attractive to him. Once again, he began to shoot at a target, and he seemed to find pleasure in it. But he wanted to make noise, to hear clatter. Then a thought came to me: we walked together through the wine cellar where many empty bottles lay. These could be shot to fragments. For a few hours, this activity became his greatest delight, but it also came to an end when there were no more bottles left. Now he had another wish: he wanted to shoot down the chandelier in the city's theater. One could readily recognize what enormous aggressions were still in the boy. That such a wish could not be fulfilled was also clear to him, and yet he would have heartily liked to break something which was still *whole*. I gave him the freedom to choose an object in our room, since I felt that his aggressions were beginning to look for a goal. The wildness, which had simply found its expression in making noise, seemed gradually to fade into the background. He looked around until his eyes fell upon a little, square, wooden table in the doll house. He asked me if he could shoot at it. "Yes you may do that," I said.

At first it might seem that the little table of the dollhouse was rather modest goal, compared to the chandelier. The square of the table meant, however, a wholeness.

Instinctively, the boy had grabbed for a symbol of wholeness; thus, he tended towards the centering, so I let him do as he pleased. What I saw behind his destructiveness might not seem evident at first glance. At this point, I would like once more to quote some thoughts from the Far East for further illustration. I thought of the spiritual meaning of archery in Japan. The art of archery is practiced there by many Zen masters, but it does not mean a bloody argument with a living opponent. It is a spiritual exercise, a dispute with oneself. When one aims at the center of the target, one aims at one's own center. In this way, the archer tries to reach his own center, often a painstaking training that lasts for years. Herrigel says of this in *Zen und die Kunst des Bogenschiessens,* (The Art of Archery): "The competition comes into existence in that the archei aims at himself—and yet not at himself—and that he might hit himself—and yet not himself—and in this way, being the aimer and the target, at the same time, is also the aggressor and the victim. Bow and arrow themselves are only a subterfuge for what could also happen without them. It is *the path* to a goal, not the goal itself."[13]

Here we clearly experience what I mentioned beforehand; i.e., that the quaternity (square table) appears when a centering, in the sense of wholeness, is sought. The boy was also an aggressor and a victim. He had to hit that aspect which hindered his development and, by doing this, hit himself. By taking this action, an old attitude was to be replaced by a new one.

A little figure belonging to the sand play was his next target. It represented a man who, in Jung's language, showed a true persona attitude—an attitude which is so perfect on the outside that it does not allow one to recognize what is going on within. He placed this little figure on a lump of clay and destroyed it completely with shots. Now he had definitely overcome this attitude which he had displayed so far. I have to admit that I had to ask myself if I had not gone too far in letting this happen. I

---

[13] Eugen Herrigel, *Zen in the Art of Archery* (New York: Pantheon Books, Inc., 1953), p. 12.

was almost afraid that he would now want to aim at living people.

The next day, I asked the father what effect this occurrence had made upon the boy. "Something very out-of-the-ordinary happened to me yesterday evening," he reported. "For the first time since earliest childhood, Kim gave me a goodnight kiss." Finally something had broken through the boy's rigid attitude. He had destroyed his mask himself. Emotions and feelings had broken through the blockade; as a result, he could embrace his father.

This moved me even more because I knew that the father himself was incapable of spontaneously showing the child his own feelings. The father was overjoyed that it was now the boy who came to him.

Thus, the moment had come when the negative aggressions had been adequately lived out. It is often not easy to recognize this turning point, but it is one of the most important moments in therapy. If the therapist misses it, there is danger that energies which had been set free will become permanently destructive. For this reason, it is extremely important that the newly awakened energies are caught by the therapist and led into constructive paths.

In the following hour, Kim discovered a blowtorch. At first, he amused himself in the garden by letting the fuel in the torch drip to the ground, so that he might light it afterwards. Many little flames were produced, and I admit it was a very amusing game. However, it was not what I was striving for in that moment, and so I guidingly interfered for the first time in this therapy.

I explained to him that the blowtorch was a very useful instrument with which one could, for example, remove old paint from wood. At that time there were still in my house, which was built in the Middle Ages, many beams that were painted with an ugly color. Together, we tried to remove the paint with the glowing jet of the blowtorch. Now this was interesting! The enthusiasm for this game, which had turned into work lasted for hours. The same energies which dissolved the paint with the flame instantly took a positive effect as the beautiful, old wood of the beams reappeared.

Now it seemed to me the moment had come for a new sand

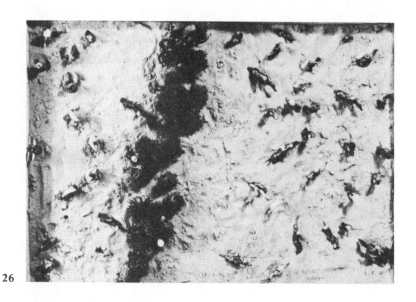

picture, and Kim himself accepted the proposal with pleasure [illustration 26]. I saw with delight that the tanks were not touched anymore. For the first time, colors, trees and people appeared in the picture. Where strong bulwarks had been erected, there now stretched a thin forest across the landscape. To the left of that—I did not trust my eyes—four Indian women with children in their arms sat around the fire.

The archetypal family situation had come to life. What had broken apart in earliest childhood had begun to unite again! What had developed in the negative for years, and whose symbol had to disappear in the form of the destruction of the square table, had now actually manifested itself in a wonderful way.

On the same side, four Indians in full-feather regalia stood in front of a totem pole, while a fight between cowboys and Indians was taking place on the other side of the little forest. "What did the Indians in front of the totem pole represent?" I asked. He answered, "They are praying that the fighting will end well for them." There is no doubt that the symbolism in this picture is the appearance of what Jung calls the Self. The four mothers, as a symbolic representation of the childlike wholeness in the most fortunate sense, showed the transformation that had happened with the boy. The limitless insecurity he was exposed to until then could now, on the basis of this solid and complete family, change into an inner security.

I was deeply touched by this happy change. From my experience, such transformation and revelation are always experienced as numinous. This was confirmed for me again in the form of the praying Indians. Life, especially in puberty, is perceived as a battle. But if this is fought based on a deep-rooted security which contains a numinous quality, it develops and strengthens the total personality.

A week later a similar picture was produced which deepened the impression on the preceding one [illustration 27]. There where formerly four Indian women had been sitting, now eight Indian figures with calumets in their mouths were surrounding the fire in a circle, while some of the Indian women were cooking and some had their children in their arms. Here, the centering had been reached.

While the number four, which represents totality, is connected in most cultures with the earth and thus points towards a

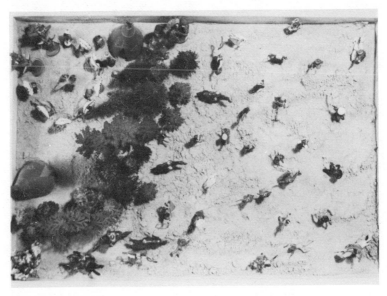

27

28

reality situation, the circle signifies the heaven as a symbol of totality and points towards the spiritual.

In my opinion, the manifestation of the Self which is represented in many forms, but most impressively in the circle, means the starting point of a healthy ego development and an unfolding of the inherent personality factors, the healthy development of the boy now seemed safeguarded to me. But its first manifestations require protection and care, like with a new-born baby. Therefore it would be wrong to dismiss a child from therapy at this moment. Potentials for development, which were earlier inhibited by fears and therefore experienced as aggressions, become free and must now be helped and directed. Then it is possible that tasks seemingly insoluble, or talents which cannot express themselves, can suddenly be approached with ease.

The many energies which had now awakened in the boy were represented in a picture for which he used two sandboxes [illustration 28]. It represented a car race in which his favorite car was in the lead. The racing cars with their strong motors personified his freed powers, which now moved safely in secured, orderly paths. Should they skid off the road, the fire brigade, Red Cross and transport trucks stood ready. But where a crashed airplane had laid in the first picture indicating a disconsolate situation, there was now a helicopter standing ready for take-off. In reality, the boy had now lived through three psychological stages, which were apparently indicated as symbolized in the number three, the form of the light weapons on the left side: Expression of the aggressions; Manifestation of the Self; A positive use of the energy sources. The goal—or, in other words, his kingdom that we wanted to reach—was on the point of being realized.

Kim found delight in constructive work. He made many friends and also became a good friend to his father, while at the same time, he started to assert himself at school. Today, six years later, and long since dismissed from therapy, he will shortly take his exams to graduate from high school, his Matura exams, and himself can answer the question which at the beginning of therapy had been so difficult to answer.

Chapter 4

DANIELA:
Separation from an Overpowering Mother Fixation

The mother described 12-year-old Daniela as shy and in-hibited, lacking the courage to visit anywhere without her mother. She was not even able to stay alone overnight with her grandmother. It was also difficult for her to make friends, thus she was quite a lonely child. Her teacher complained of her lack of interest and participation in school activities. In spite of the fact that she was tall for her age and physically well developed, she gave the impression of being a totally passive pupil, unfit for the academic high school level to which she had been as-signed. The school proposed putting the child through a less demanding course of study. Because the parents were very disturbed at this proposal, they brought her to me for observa-tion.

Willingly, Daniela agreed to my suggestion that she play with the figures in my collection [illustration 29]. She started, as she said, by letting cows graze in a fenced pasture. In front of the pasture was a coach that was pulled by two horses whose hooves were stuck deep in the sand. Directly in front of the horses a street was marked off, leading to an inn on the op-posite side. A man was walking towards the inn. By the street, under a tree was a bench for resting.

It seemed apparent that Daniela's coach of life had come to a standstill. The horses could go forward only with the greatest of difficulty; their hooves were stuck near the motherly sphere represented by the grazing cows. The path into the world seemed long and tiring. This was represented by the inn, the place which is open to any visitor. Since this was placed on the opposite left hand corner, it indicated that the child should come in contact with her unconscious—with, so to speak, her own inner sources. This was necessary to enable her to ex-, perience an adequate development. At the inn stood a male figure who, contrary to the mother who embodied the world at home represented the girl's relationship to the outer world.

29

Although Daniela gave the impression of being overly introverted, right from the start she seemed at ease with me. Therefore, I suggested to the parents that they have their daughter undergo a short-termed therapy. I planned to attempt freeing the girl of her inhibitions.

In the second hour, she reported that she had had a "gruesome" dream involving snakes, and that she could not forget it. I suggested to her that she draw or paint these snakes, since alarming things often lose some of their power to frighten when one tries to reproduce them. She started the task immediately, and with a sure hand, she drew eight snakes which were dispersed in the meadow. She colorfully painted them with watercolors; the meadow was a luscious green, strewn with flowers. Daniela thought that the picture gave a rather gay impression. A slowworm rolled up in itself, was the only snake tinted gray. It might represent the problem still lying wholly in the unconscious, still a fully undeveloped, colorless female side of the girl's being. The snake often appears during puberty, when the transformation to adulthood reaches deeper layers.

30

31

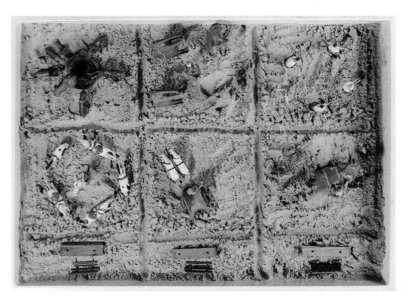

32

The shedding of the snake's skin symbolizes a renewal being prepared in the unconscious. It animates the secret of life.

I try to interpret dreams, as well as sand pictures for the child, on the level of her conscious understanding. For this reason, I asked Daniela what number of subjects she had at school. Eight was the answer! All of them, except mathematics, she said, she managed passably. We found that of the eight snakes, the single coiled serpent represented the most disliked subject, and that from now on, most of her attention had to be paid to it. With that, the dream lost its menacing aspect to Daniela.

Her second sand picture, represented a traffic jam at an intersection [illustration 30]. From four sides, cars approached the intersection. However, the street was too narrow and it seemed impossible for them to pass. Only the ambulance which was right at the intersection, could get through, Daniela explained. What was striking was the fact that a majority of cars came from the left as they drove through a street lined with trees. One could assume that blocked energies in the unconscious were already being set in motion. This idea was supported by a gasoline station at the lower left corner of the picture, where the motors were refueled with new energies. The whole character of the picture seemed to give a hopeful indication that these onrushing new energies could be disciplined in therapy, and that she could overcome her passivity. (The ambulance was coming to the rescue.)

From the third picture, it could be seen that the energies of life had indeed started flowing [illustration 31]. A wide stream crossed the landscape; a bridge over which cars could pass, connected both shores. To the left was the inn, but now it could be reached by automobiles. Daniela brought relatively large stones out of the garden and placed them in the river. The flowing water indicated that the restraints in the child had started to dissolve, but the stones signified the obstacles that were still to be overcome. On the other hand, this same picture reminded me of a Chinese description of water which is in the I Ching [Book of Changes]: "The water flows uninterruptedly and reaches the goal. It flows and does not accumulate anywhere. It does not lose its reliable nature at the dangerous places either."

This gave confidence for the future—especially since Daniela had also become much more active in her daily life. She met occasionally with friends and invited them to visit her at home. She found pleasure in doing handicrafts, and liked above all to paint and draw, in which she showed talent.

In the fourth picture, she depicted a circus [illustration 32]. The whole space was divided into six squares, in each of which a performance was taking place. In the upper left, tigers and lions performed their tricks. The tiger was leaving the podium while a lion was on the point of ascending it. In the adjoining area, the trainer occupied himself with four elephants. In the upper corner, five ballerinas formed a circle. White horses circled around one who stood in the middle at the bottom left. In the next section was a Roman chariot, and on the bottom right of the sandbox, clowns were doing their tricks. On the very bottom, benches were arranged for the audience.

The different representations in the squares all aimed towards the centering, or represented a circumambulation: the tiger, appearing with the lion, had to be viewed as the female, shadow aspect of the lion. The Latin word: *tigris*, the tiger, is of the female gender and stands for the dark womanliness. The lion, as the king of the animals, is associated with the sun because of his yellow coat. The symbol alludes to a clearing up of the conscious mind; its vitality speaks for energies which are ready to awaken. Since the tiger was descending from the podium in the center and the lion was on the point of ascending it, we can assume that a transformation in the development of the child was indicated. This would lead to a vitalizing of the energy forces that had, until then, slumbered in the child. This vitality was also expressed in the elephants of the adjoining section which are a general symbol for strength and intelligence.

The true femininity of the girl was expressed in the dance of the ballerinas. Walter F. Otto says in *Der Tanz* (The Dance): "Dances were originally the spontaneous expression of deeply stirred emotions where the cause and the result of the emotions become one."[14] The dancing person crystallizes into his own essence; into his divine evolution. The circle of dancers indicated not merely femininity but also contact with the inner deity that lives in every human being. The circle has always been

14 Walter F. Otto, *Menschengestalt und Tanz* (Munich: Hermann Rinn, 1956).

the expression for that very great experience that has been associated with the divine.

The 12-year-old girl seemed to have presented a deep inner experience here that could never have been put into words.

Horses are animals with an excellent instinct; since they carry the rider, they also have a maternal aspect. White horses are heavenly horses and are near the gods. For this reason, the white horses encircling the one in the middle, standing on its hind legs, might express a still unconscious religious motion in the child.

The Roman chariots reminded one of the original meaning of the circus. *Kirkos* is Greek and means circle. Here, also, a circular movement is indicated.

The clown is the jester who possesses a thorough knowlege of all artistic disciplines. Behind his jests hides profound, universal wisdom which must be perceived and understood by every individual. This might refer to the development of Daniela's personality. Normally this follows a period of inner peace, which the child had expressed in the circular movements around the central point.

Illustration 33, done a few weeks later, showed that this assumption had been correct. In the meantime, Daniela's work and general participation in school activities improved substantially.

This picture shows five women who are coming to the village well to fetch water. (Well: The big roof that appears above the little forest). On the left stands a man. A path with a bridge over it leads to the nearby village. In contrast to the five ballerinas moving in a circle [illustration 32], who made it possible to assume a numinous experience, these five women are carrying out an everyday chore. Here, rather, the natural womanliness is now represented: the woman who provides for the nutrition and the welfare of her family. This belongs to that phase of growth in which the transformation from girl to woman takes place, and in which the ego is strengthened.

Here, Daniela had now reached the source of the unconscious, as had been prognosticated in the first picture. It was the source of her nature, previously concealed, but now brought to surface. The action of drawing water from the well is, like catching a fish, a symbolic action: through it, contents from the depth of the unconscious are brought to light.

The figure of the man standing somewhat to the side is seen as the male aspect of the girl's being. He has now assumed his important place in the formation of her pesonality.

I have, again and again, observed that the other side of the being in man becomes positively activated right after the centering experience. Only then can the relationship to the collective—to the outer world—be formed.

Daniela, whose school problems were now solved and whose relationship to her mother had been eased, dedicated herself to drawing. She made posters indicating that the growing young girl was turning more and more to the outer world.

Finally, she proved her readiness to leave the parental nest in the last sand picture [illustration 34]. On an airfield, airplanes were standing ready to take off, ships rode at anchor ready to sail away, a mail coach and a car stood ready to start, and a train was on a point of beginning to move. All were ready—in the water, on the land and in the air—to explore the four points of the compass.

33

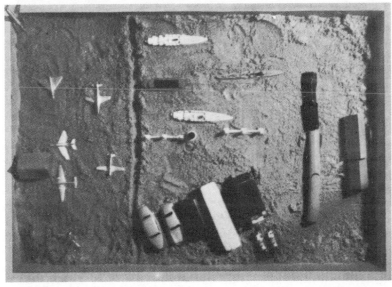

34

/ 83

Chapter 5

CHRISTIAN:
Healing of an Enuresis

Generally we know that it is very difficult to cure enuresis; it is especially difficult when the child has reached an age when he or she should have outgrown bed-wetting a long time ago. Therefore, I had great doubt when a mother, who lived far away from my city, phoned me to ask if I could help her 12-year-old son get rid of this problem during an eight-day vacation. I finally gave in to her urgent request and agreed to see the boy in my office for consultation. I hoped to be able to get to the root of this complaint. During his vacation, the boy would stay with relatives who lived close to me.

Christian was a very bright sixth-grade pupil. He appeared to be somewhat inhibited in the presence of his mother, who was the authority in the family, in contrast to the rather indulgent father. The boy however relaxed immediately as we entered the playroom together.

Since I hoped to diagnose his illness as fast as possible and if possible to give a prognosis, I immediately asked the boy to make a picture in the sand with my figures. This is not my usual procedure. Obviously pleased—yet somewhat doubtful that this would help him to get rid of his unpleasant habit—he followed my suggestion. While he looked at the figures, he started to talk. He told me that he suffered greatly from bed-wetting. Several doctors already had been consulted, but no remedy had been found. He would always awaken after it was too late to go to the toilet. They even tried a complicated mechanism to wake him up in time, but this had not worked either.

I felt sorry for him when he confided his difficulty to me; he evidently suffered very much. Again he shook his head—he

/ 84

could not understand how this sandplay could help him. I explained to him that I might be able to discover the roots of his problem from his sand picture: that this knowledge was based on long and thorough studies I had made; and that when I could discover the cause of his trouble, I might be able to help him. I further explained to him that we have much in us we do not know anything about. Sometimes these could be "good ideas" which could be helpful; sometimes they could be "bad ideas" causing disturbances. Such images would come to the surface while he played in the sand, and I hoped to be able to detect whether they had anything to do with his bed-wetting.

Wondering about this, he looked at me and started to choose some figures. With his hand, he drew a kind of oval in the sand, which he populated with soldiers and crusaders (illustration 35). He stated that, they were fighting with each other, and separated them with a high fence. They were shot at from the outside by other soldiers. A wounded man was carried away on a stretcher. Some Englishmen stood nearby, not participating in the battle.

35

36

37

38

He said they would help to bring peace. However at a midway point near the upper rim of the sandbox, he placed a pelican.

From this picture, I could easily perceive the opposing fighting energies inside this boy. They produced insecurity, and therefore he felt threatened from the outside. He even imagined himself as a wounded soldier (soldier on a stretcher); as one who was hurt and had to give up the fight. The situation however was not hopeless, for the Englishmen would achieve peace, Christian said. He could not tell me why only the English would be able to bring peace about; he just remarked that he liked them very much.

For my interpretation, I had to resort to the generally accepted characteristics of Englishmen. The character of the English people has been molded by their insular location and the stability of their society. The English appear to be self-confident and balanced. The whole world knows the general concepts of "gentlemen" and "fair play." They demonstrate a character development which plays an important role in the English educational system, in addition to the knowledge their students acquire at school. One could deduce from this that the boy longed for an inner stability. But what was the meaning of the pelican which watched over the whole proceedings? A pelican is a symbol of mother love. According to an ancient legend, it tears open its breast to nourish its young ones with its own blood. Did this mean that Christian unconsciously expected the restoration of his inner peace to be under the protection of a mother-child unity? Everything pointed towards a mother-related problem.

Christian's mother told me that she had the whole responsibility of the upbringing of her four boys. She had to discipline and teach them orderliness, because the father was completely consumed by his profession. Therefore, he spoiled the children during the rare times they were together.

The next day, Christian made another sand picture [illustration 36], which provided even more insight into this problem. It represented a circus, in the arena of which was an animal trainer with his four tame tigers. In the center, Christian posted a lamp with four arms—a very unusual item for a circus arena. Spectators were all around; on the left there were artists, clowns and Roman chariots ready to perform.

It became clear to me that Christian experienced his mother's education as "taming." The mother had to assume the role of the father with a lot of strength and energy and in good faith, but he missed the warmth from his overly conscientious mother.

I tried, therefore, to follow him completely. He started to feel at home with me and wanted to play with other materials. Since it was close to Christmas, he wanted to use this opportunity to make some Christmas presents. He started work with clay, and he succeeded in making a bowl very well; later he wanted to paint it. He became gay and alive, and I was happy to see his liberation after he had constructed two sand pictures in which he had unconsciously communicated his problems to me.

After he had worked on his handicrafts for two more mornings, he made another sand picture. This one was completely different [illustration 37]. With great care, he built a broad road with an underpass. This was rather difficult to do, for it needed an elaborate, wood construction so that he could put sand on top of it to form a firm, solid road. Heavy traffic in both directions was regulated by a strong, visible stripe in the middle of the road. The street which led to the underpass was also bustling with traffic that was directed by police. This showed that the boy's aggressive energies, portrayed in the first picture, were now well-ordered and had lost their aggressiveness.

The pelican in the first picture was replaced—yet on the opposing side—by a nurse. Christian had experienced my complete acceptance of him and, therefore, felt as secure as in the protection of a caring mother. This had started to have a healing influence on him.

The following day he again played with other materials. When he was very busy building a small airplane for his brother, he suddenly said, "Mrs. Kalff, you know more than a doctor."

"How do you mean that?" I asked.

"I have not wet my bed now for two nights," he answered.

I was very glad for him and hoped quietly that the bed-wetting would not recur. He had gotten rid of the doubt that sandplay could be as helpful as the pills—which he equated with the help from a doctor. There seemed to be some success in my treatment, and I discussed with Christian the possibility of getting permission from his teacher to extend his stay here. He loved this idea and we received an extension of eight days. Christian came daily and continued to make Christmas presents for everyone, his brothers and parents. We never discussed his bed-wetting, but one day he repeated, while shaking his head, "It is really true—you know more than doctors."

His bed remained dry. He spoke about his brothers and parents, and I felt his closeness to them. He felt secure enough to hope for a most wonderful event to happen—that he could go with his friends on a skiing trip after New Year's day. Up until now, he had had to stay at home because of his bed-wetting.

He could not stay more than two weeks. The last day, I asked him to make another sand picture [illustration 38]. Again, it represented a circus, but this time the English were the actors in the arena. Now they represented his inner peace. I could scarcely believe it myself. A transformation had apparently taken place in this short time. I feared the sudden interruption of our intimate relationship might produce a regression. When he said goodbye to me, he again whispered into my ear, "You really know more than a doctor."

For a while, he phoned every week, and slowly the intervals of our contact became longer and longer, until they finally stopped.

JAMES:
Loss of Instinct
Due to an Identification
With an Extroverted Mother

Sixteen-year-old James was exceptionally tall for his age. His shoulders were as broad as a man's and his manners were more those of an adult than of a child. He smoked incessantly and carried on a lively conversation. His motto was: have as many friends as possible in order never to be alone.

He was the second oldest of five children. His entire family had come from the United State to live in Europe for a year. The children were to attend German-speaking schools to have a closer contact with the people and culture of a different continent. It was easy to foresee that James, who had had problems in America with learning and concentration in high school, and who barely could manage the requirements of his high school curriculum, would fail in a foreign school. Above all, his English did not correspond with the norm for his age. It seemed out of the question that he would be accepted for admission by a college. For this reason, the parents asked me to let the boy live with me during their first part of their stay in Europe.

The great unrest which dominated James was immediately expressed . He could not be alone, nor could he occupy himself with any activity. This caused him to lead a very extroverted life: he went to a movie almost everyday or met with others in a café. To be "at home" was torment for him. It was at once evident to me, however, that his extroversion was not genuine. The gestures that accompanied his conversations revealed a helplessness which was also evident in his gait—which, despite an apparent nimbleness, was rather heavy. His feet seemed to cling to the floor as though they sought to find a foothold on the ground. What was the underlying cause that was hiding behind his adult facade?

At the beginning of therapy, he produced a sand picture representing a rural scene [illustration 39]: a farm with geese, chickens, a sow with her young; a farmer who sowed his newly plowed field; two horses, one light and one dark in an enclosure; blossoming trees and grazing cows. The terrain traversed a little stream that emptied at the left into a lake. The whole picture gave a very peaceful impression. I asked myself if it was an expression of the boy's longing for being close to nature.

39

And yet two things struck me: first, in the field, where the cows were grazing near the luscious, green trees, stood a small, leafless tree on which two ravens were sitting. The mother cow, which gives milk, symbolized the nourishing mother in many earlier cultures—in Mesopotamia, in Egypt, in China and, still today, in India. Therefore, the realm of the grazing cows in our picture could readily be looked upon as that of motherliness. Since the leafless little tree was right in the range of the grazing cows, I was inclined to assume that something must have been disturbed in the child-mother relationship. Consequently, I asked James's mother if any experience or serious illness had taken place during the first year of his life which could have had an influence on his development. She remembered the following:

When James was nine months old, he had had bronchitis, which was treated with inhalations. Through careless handling of the inhalator, the crib had caught fire. Luckily, the baby was not seriously burned and had only a little scar on the forehead as a result. However, I assumed that this experience had produced a shock in James. considering that at this tender age the child normally lives wholly within the mother-child unity, this shock was effective enough to have a disturbing effect on this relationship. Was it possible that the experience had an effect on James, who at this tender age was still living unconsciously? Further clues would have to be found to establish that conclusion. Secondly, there were two horses completely enclosed by a fence, which had no opening, no gate. The symbolism of the horse has many layers and must be seen from different angles. First of all, the horse is a symbol of the instinctual sphere. On this level, it is closely connected with man in the relationship of horse and rider. In fairy tales, the horse leads the lost prince home. The horse is often mentioned as being clairaudient and clairvoyant. These capabilities make it a *psychopompos* (a leader of lost souls). As a dark horse it is associated with Poseidon, the Greek god of the sea who, according to the myth, stirs the sea with his trident. The winged horse of Greek mythology is Pegasus who opens the spring, Hippocrene, with his hoof. For this reason, the capability of bringing the unconscious (water) to light is attributed to him. Horses further symbolize psychic energies, because of their fast gait and their intensity (horsepower).

The white horse is connected with light—with the sun. White horses pulled the chariot of Helios, and a white horse carried the Chinese monk to India. The monk returned with Buddha's scriptures to China, where a temple was dedicated to the horse. The white horse can also be found in the Christian tradition as well as Chinese. In the Bible's *Book of Revelations,* 19:11, it says that Christ will ride on a white horse in order to fight the two evil animals that will come out of the nether world.

Since the two horses, a dark one and a light one, were completely isolated from the rest of the farm, it was easy to presume that a loss of instinct was chiefly to be blamed for the boy's onesided development. He could not attend school in his condition, and yet it seemed desirable to me that he should get somewhat acquainted with the German language. A student undertook the task of tutoring him. However, it seemed to me that the most important thing was to try to provide him access to his instincts. Since he loved animals, I inquired at the zoo about a position for him as a volunteer. We were lucky: he had just passed the prescribed age of sixteen; he also carried the proper insurance.

He went to the zoo two or three afternoons a week to clean the monkey cages and after doing his work, to watch the animals. This task was evidently fun for him. Little by little, the animals recognized him and challenged him to play with them. One was very fond of James and reacted affectionately to him.

In order to orient myself about James's school level, I looked through his schoolbooks. The torn books gave the impression of belonging to a boy who was bored and, as a result, had scribbled all over the margins. In the last blank page I discovered a small drawing by James that represented Christ on the cross; however, this male figure had no penis. James could not have represented his situation more clearly: he saw himself as crucified, since his masculinity had not been able to develop. In fact, he seemed very attached to his mother. He was her favorite son; he was so entirely devoted to her that his own being had not been able to develop.

A dream which James related to me confirmed my apprehensions. He had dreamed that the path which led to his house was lined to the left by crocodiles. Crocodiles have a threatening, aggressive, even devouring aspect. Jung mentions, in *Symbols of Transformation,* that the theriomorphic symbols always apply to the unconscious libido manifestations that either belong in general to the unconscious or point to the suppression of the instincts. He says further: "These are the vital foundations, the laws governing all life. The regression caused by repressing the instincts always leads back to the psychic past, and consequently to the phase of childhood where the decisive factors appear to be, and sometimes actually are, the parents".[15]

The boy stood in danger of being attacked and devoured by the crocodiles. In order to encounter them, it was necessary that he come in contact with his instinctual sphere. I hoped that his relationship with the animals, especially with the apes that had become his friends in the zoo, would result in an encounter with those energies which still slumbered deep in his unconscious. Only when he got to know that energy would he be able to place it at his disposal! Since the crocodile lives in the water and on the land, it represents a connection between the unconscious and consciousness.

Now that he was separated for the first time from the emphatically extroverted mother who controlled all his actions, it was frightfully difficult for James to orient himself. Yet he quickly became happy in our house and tried to adapt himself to our habits. I attached great importance to reliance upon his own views in order to give rise to a feeling of his real self. The tutoring that he had been receiving almost daily soon helped him so much that he could converse a little in German. He could not and did not want to write, not even in English, for it caused him extraordinary effort and his writing was practically illegible. Only unwillingly did he bend to the proposal of writing down a dream or an experience. But later he visibly calmed down and began to also show interest in his own language.

Two months later, James came home and said, "I told the zoo director that I was not going to work at the zoo any longer." I was somewhat astounded by the decision he had made on his own, yet I respected it. When I asked him what he wanted to undertake, he answered, "I want to go to school." This was even more surprising; however, we immediately discussed the question of which school, since he still had to accustom himself to the German language. Within a few days he went, as an auditor, to a private school, while he continued the German classes with increased effort. At that time, he produced a sand picture which indicated the unexpected change in his condition [illustration 40].

15 C. G. Jung, *Symbols of Transformation,* Collected Works, Vol. 5 (New York: Pantheon Books, Inc., 1967), p. 180.

40

In the lower left corner, he built a small village out of which led a rather wide path across the picture towards the top. A girl was driving some geese home, and a shepherd was about to take the young lambs out of the fold and bring them to the sheeps pen. Grazing sheep, a horse and a cow were walking towards the village. It was evening. A small group was moving on the path to the village. A man and woman walked with a donkey. I asked James if these people had any meaning. He said they were Mary and Joseph, who were on their way to the village because Mary was about to give birth to a child.

This statement moved me deeply! Was it possible that James, who was apparently only thinking of getting away from himself, was already on the path to finding himself? Was the child that was to be born his own new situation? Was he himself going to be "newly born"? There were some signs—e.g., in the way he spoke of his friends, the animals in the zoo or how he had established his relationship to me—left no doubt in my mind that James was about to approach a centering in the un-conscious, the way in which it takes place in a small child.

Even though the birth of Christ represents a one-time historic happening, it has an archetypal character. "Christ is the Son of the Father," states Jung. "He is the Logos, the *Judex Mundi*, Saviour and Redeemer, an all-embracing totality. As a shepherd he is the leader and the center of the flock. He is more complete and more perfect than the natural person. He surpasses and encompasses man, who is to him what a child is to an adult, or an animal (sheep) to a human being."[16] Young James had expressed in this picture the approach to his own inner religiosity. According to his tradition, it carried a Christian character even though his religiosity had not been consciously nurtured.

James was on the path of rendering himself into the hands of an archetypal figure of the mother. It was Mary, the mother of God, who in the picture, was on her way to the birth. The shepherd was also about to bring the young sheep into safety before nightfall. The evening calm and preparation for the night, where the great event was going to take place, was also a sign of a significant introversion, and a time of readiness for the deeper regions of the unconscious in James.

James was now given an assignment to write either a diary or a story of his choice every day. This was to give him practice in English, which was very poor. Over a period of time he wrote a story of a young man named Tol, who left his family to go into the woods, armed only with a knife. I want to quote the principal part of the story here, word for word:

> Tol stopped a moment to watch the sun slowly creep over the tree tops. Half-smiling, he picked up his knife and trotted on down the hill. Upon reaching the bottom, he branched off to the left, preferring the shelter of the trees to that of the open plain. He walked quickly, hoping to reach a small stream soon, for he was thirsty. After going a half mile, he suddenly stopped. Changing directions, he moved slowly on. He had gone only a few yards when he stopped again. Frowning slightly, he moved on a little faster. After going several yards, he halted abruptly. This

---

[16] C. G. Jung, *Psychology and Religion,* Collected Works, Vol. 11 (New York: Pantheon Books, Inc., 1967), p. 155.

time there was no mistaking it! The sound of men! Soon the air became stagnant with their smell. He quickly sprang to the safety of a lowhanging branch and then climbed up higher. The men soon came into view, shuffling along in single file. They marched past Tol's tree, then went out of sight. As soon as they were gone, Tol jumped down from the tree and darted off in the opposite direction. He ran until he had shaken off the sound and smell of them. Slowing down, he changed directions until he was parallel to the direction in which the men were going. He then kept up a steady trot until midmorning, when he came upon a small stream. Stopping only long enough to get a drink, he moved on.

He travelled the rest of the morning in peace, stopping only once to get a drink of water. By noon he was feeling very hungry, so he veered to the left and stepped out into a large plain. He stood in the tall grass for awhile, getting use to the bright light and at the same time looking for food. After a time he spotted a small gazelle a little away from the main herd. The wind was favorable and he was able to get within a knife's throw of it. In almost the same movement, he threw the knife and chased after his prize. It was still kicking when he got to it, but he swiftly broke its neck. Carefully, he cut off a piece and began to eat it. After eating all he needed to fulfill his hunger, he lay down on the grass to sleep, but before falling asleep his thoughts were, as always, of home.

Twenty days later:

Falling asleep, Tol began to dream. He walked up to the path to the cave and saw his wife sitting at the entrance, playing with their seven-year-old son, Ruk. Upon reaching the top of the hill, he looked around. The trees were just beginning to turn green, and the sweet fragrance of new flowers was in the air. Down in the valley, he could see the movement of large animals as they plowed through the thick undergrowth. Here was the best hunting ground to be found within fifty miles. There were gazelles, bears, great mammoth, and birds of all kinds. Fruit and water were near. His chest swelled in pride as he beheld all of this. This was his home, his will to live, and his very life. All that he could want or need was here. He turned around and called out to his wife and son, who were still unaware of his presence. Ruk, getting to him first, wrapped his small arms around his father's neck, while his wife, a little slower, greeted him with tears in her eyes.

Still in the process of waking up, Tol could hear the joy of his wife and child over his return. Very reluctantly, he got up and started on his way again.

Fourteen days later:

Tol travelled the rest of the afternoon in comparative peace. As darkness of night came over the earth, he began to hunt for a tree in which to sleep. After a long and hard search he found an old, strong tree to climb up for shelter. He went up as far as he could then lay across a thick branch. As he lay there waiting for sleep to come, he tried to distinguish the different sounds of night: the loud and shrill cry of a pterodactyl flying around looking for food; the grunts of a tyrannosaur sleeping nearby; the voices and grunts of the smaller animals as they ran through the night in their endless quest for food.

He thought back over the days and weeks he had spent in search of Kezz, the horse. He had first seen him two weeks ago near the cave and had been trailing him ever since. But the trail had been lost when he had gone beyond the mountains. He had then been forced to turn toward home, where his wife and child patiently waited for him.

Soon his thoughts were only a confused jumble of ideas, and then he went to sleep.

Seven days later:

Waking early, Tol climbed out of his tree and stood in the sunlight listening to the birds high up in the treetops. How much difference there was between the sounds of night and those of the early morning! The morning was filled with the optimism of a new day, while the night was

full of the sounds of struggle and labouring. The morning
so intoxicated him that he had the urge to cry out to the
world. Instead, he ran wildly through the bush without
knowing where he was going. Quite suddenly he came
upon a small lake, and jumped right in. He enjoyed the
cool water for awhile, then sat down on the shore to dry
off. A short while later he saw a large head, followed by a
snake-like neck, emerge from the water. The creature took
a deep breath, then, with a loud hiss, sank back into the
water. Having recovered. Tol began looking for food.
Slowly, he crept to the water. He stood bent over the water
for quite some time, until he saw the fish he wanted. With
unbelievable speed he dived after it, but the fish was faster
still and vanished. He tried three more times, but without
success.

On the fourth try, he was able to grab a fair-sized one,
which he promptly knocked against a tree. Afterwards he
rubbed it on a rock to scrape off the scales. Then he pulled
the meat off the bones and, without great hurry, ate it in
three bites. He then washed his mouth, picked up his knife
and started off. The morning was marvelous! He felt like a
dwarf as he ran between the trunks of the trees. Their tops
were swathed in fog while the lower branches were covered
by thick, green moss. He had the distinct feeling of being
in a land of giants.

While Tol ran through the forest, other creatures were
moving around him. A large brontosaurus was chewing
grass. Nearby, a small deer broke through the bushes; it
was being pursued by a wolfish-looking animal. A
pterodactyl flew overhead, looking for smaller animals. A
wild tiger stood on a high rock and screamed its de-
fiance to the world. Far off, he heard the last cry of a
small animal caught in the paw of a larger one.

None of this did Tol notice consciously, but rather all
of it penetrated into his unconscious. When he heard the
sound of a larger animal, he changed directions according to wherever the noise originated. This did not,
however, always work. Once, he blundered through the
bushes upon a tyrannosaur and was lucky not to be torn
between its jaws.

As he went along, his thoughts were turning over in an effort to figure out a way to capture the horse. He knew that when he saw him again, he would have only one chance; for if he failed and hurt him in any way, there could be no hope of ever capturing him. Abruptly, his train of thought stopped. He was not sure what was interfering, but there was something wrong. He stopped short. There in front of him was his horse, gleaming white in the morning sun. He was just twenty feet away, but Tol was sure that it had not sensed his presence. Very slowly, the horse approached. When the animal was within ten feet Tol quickly tried to devise a way to capture him. What he wanted to do most was to put him in some sort of enclosure, but he did not have the time to make one. For awhile, he was completely undecided as to what to do. Then thinking over the last days of his journey, he remembered a small valley that might be used as an enclosure. The big problem now was how to get the horse to it. By getting behind him and letting him smell his scent, Tol might be able to frighten him just enough to push him in the right direction. However Tol did not want to scare the horse, for he might flee to the mountains.

Ever so slowly, Tol crept around behind the horse, taking great care not to step on any branches. At last he was able to get directly behind him. Cautiously, he moved toward the horse. At first, the horse took no notice; but when he got nearer, the horse stopped grazing. As Tol came up closer, the horse moved away. This went on for about three hours until Tol was able to see the opening of the canyon, but he was afraid that the horse would not enter; but, as Tol approached the animal it gave no sign of being afraid of the trap to which he was led. Quite suddenly, the horse moved on the rocky path that led into the canyon. As soon as the horse was inside, Tol began throwing branches across the entrance. The horse was his!

Now that he had the horse, Tol had to find a way in which to tame him. Tol knew that after he had trapped the horse, the animal would not trust him because he had been robbed of his freedom. To tame him, he must first show the horse that he wanted to be his friend. Therefore, every morning he would bring small treats to the horse in the hope that he would be able to build up trust between them. At first, Kezz would become frightened and run to the far end of the canyon; but gradually, Tol was able to stroke him while the horse nibbled small tidbits from his hand. After several days, when Tol whistled, Kezz would gallop to him.

Many days went by before Tol decided that it was time to try the next step, which was to enter the corral with the horse. Very early in the morning, Tol crawled under the gate and stood next to the horse. Kezz stood a moment, looking at his new friend, then trotted to the other end of the corral. Slowly, Tol walked toward him holding a large fruit in his hand and talked very softly. The horse stood for a moment, undecided as to whether to run away or stay. Finally, he decided to stay, and he allowed Tol to stroke his neck. Every day after that Tol would enter the corral with Kezz, but never tried to get onto his back for fear of losing the trust he had built up so cautiously.

Several weeks passed and Tol knew that sooner or later he must try to mount Kezz. He chose a fine spring morning and went to the corral earlier than usual. As soon as he was close to Kezz, the horse knew that something unusual was about to happen. Tol started talking to him and at the same time, tried to get up on the horse's back. Slowly he mounted it. During all this time Kezz had stood perfectly still; but as soon as he felt Tol's weight on his back, he reared up and threw off Tol, who landed on the ground with a hard thump. Slowly, Tol got up and walked over to the horse, which had run to the far end of the corral. Again he talked softly to the horse, again he eased upon its back, and once more he was thrown off. Undaunted, he tried again and again, and with each try, the horse would buck less and less, until finally Tol was able to trot around the corral without being thrown off. The horse was tamed! Tol jumped off, opened the gate of the cor-

ral, and let Kezz out. He whistled, and Kezz came back.
This was the beginning of a long and true friendship
between horse and man, which was to last for centuries.

In the story of Tol, James had described his own way of discovering his inner self. He had let the outside world and had gone to the steppe and the primeval forest, i.e., to the deepest layers of his unconscious. He described very well how he avoided people; he wanted and had to be, alone with himself. He had been oriented only to the outside for too long a time, without knowing which energies slumbered within him. Step by step, he had described the approach to the sphere of his animal instinct as symbolized by the animals of the steppe and primeval forest. At first, he avoided them; later, driven by hunger, he had to learn how to deal with them. He hunted a wild animal, a gazelle and ate enough of it to appease his hunger. The gazelle, in myth, stands for a picture of the soul—a shy, fugitive animal that is constantly in flight from the beast of prey. It showed me clearly how much James was threatened by overwhelming, aggressive instinct.

By eating until his hunger was quieted, he integrated much of his threatened, primitive self, so that he was able to be on his guard and not fall between the teeth of a beast of prey.

Strengthened by a deep sleep in the branches of a tree, on the following day he came to a small lake where he had to exert a great effort to catch a fish. To protect himself from the unfavorable devouring influences of his earlier surroundings, he had to fish his own hidden contents out of the unconscious (water). He had, indeed, already indicated he was to be reborn in the sand picture that represented the impending birth of Christ. "The fish in dreams," says Jung in his *Symbols of Transformation* "occasionally signifies the unborn child, because the child before its birth lives in the water like a fish."[17]

The fish which was caught and eaten by Tol was indeed great significance on James's development, for it was taken out of the depths of the unconscious. James was thus en-

---

[17] C. G.Jung, *Symbols of Transformation,* Collected Works, Vol. 5 (New York: Pantheon Books, Inc., 1967), p. 198.

riched with the contents that the fish embodies. The fish is also a fertility symbol because of its many eggs. Could it be assumed that James was hiding an unknown treasure within?

But, above all, the fish is a symbol of Christ. Christ was often called by the name $ἰχθΰ$, (the Greek word for fish whose letters spell $Ἰησους,$ $χριστος$ $θεγῦ$ $υἱς$ $σωτὐρ$. Jung says that for this reason, the fish symbol represents the bridge between the historic shape of Christ and the spiritual nature of man, in which the archetype of the saviour reposes.

James had sought, completely unconsciously, for a deliverance from his condition; a way now began to emerge from the depths of his unconscious. Even more, it seemed as if the Self was beginning to become evident as it is in the pattern of the early-childhood level.

After he had caught the fish and eaten it as in a ritual, he discovered the tall trees which made a person feel very small. This part reminded me of a statement of the old Zen master, Suzuki. He said: "Western man wants to overcome Nature while Eastern man feels like a tiny part of her."

Only now was James really close to the earth. Animals crept through the thicket; and, in his joy over the magnificent morning in nature, he suddenly remembered the horse that he had planned to capture. It was not long before he discovered it: "There, in front of him was his horse, gleaming white in the morning sun..."

The security that James had gained by his approach to his own nature made it possible for him, with great caution, to catch the horse and to summon enough patience to tame it.

I was deeply touched by his words: "This was the beginning of a long and true friendship between horse and man." With that he had gained access to his instinctual sphere, which corresponded to a rebirth.

James had understood that the attitude of his unconsciousness, molded by arbitrary opinions, had been completely one-sided, and that he had been led astray by it. Only on the matrix of his own instincts could he develop his individuality.

At that time, he told me the following dream: "I was somehow together with my parents, in search for Easter eggs. The peculiar thing was that we didn't find eggs, but presents.

Contrary to my usual habit, I was nice to my sister. She had received a horse and wagon which she wanted to drive around. However, I asked her if I could guide the horse. She agreed and thus I drove my sister around in he wagon."

One of the most important Easter traditions is giving Easter eggs, symbols of fertility. Now there was no more doubt that James was advancing toward a more fruitful period. In the dream, the parents were present. However, they did not participate in the action. James himself now drove the horse that pulled his sister's wagon. The mother anima had lost power; while his sister's, a younger anima image, had gained new significance. The sister now became the source of new life. Jung says about this transition, in *Psychology and Alchemy:* "This is really a normal life process, but it usually takes place quite unconsciously. The anima is an archetype that is always present. The mother is the first bearer of the anima image, which gives her a fascinating quality in the eyes of the son. It is then transferred, via the sister and similar figures, to the beloved."[18]

James's transition was also clearly noticeable in everyday life. He expressed the wish to attend school as a student instead of auditing classes. For this objective, we changed schools once again, so that here, too, a new beginning would lend importance to what had happened. We registered for all the subjects that would enable James to pass the college entrance examination within a reasonable amount of time. Even though the German language was still a handicap, he applied himself diligently to his studies and worked a great deal on his homework.

Soon he found a girlfriend and, even though he was now almost always at home, he only allowed himself to go out once a week! His life turned out to be much richer for him.

One day he asked me spontaneously, "Mrs. Kalff, do you believe in God?" I told him that I not only believed, but that I had also experienced His existence. This was the beginning of conversations of religious and philosophic nature.

When we seriously work with juveniles, we experience that

---

[18] C. G. Jung, *Psychology and Alchemy,* Collected Works, Vol. 12 (New York: Pantheon Books, Inc., 1953), p. 70

in puberty, besides the physical development, a spiritual deepening occurs. With many primitive people, the passages from one stage of life to another, especially that from child to man, were given consecration through extended ceremonies. Today, these have to a large extent disappeared, or they have lost their deep meaning. For this reason, it is therefore much more important in therapy, especially with juveniles, to deal with the question of God. Only in the relationship to the archetype of the divine in man can the juvenile really accomplish the transformation to adulthood. This, in turn, appears when man has a natural access to his instinctual sphere.

A picture that James made in the sand about three months later confirmed by insights. It again represented a landscape [illustration 41]. To the left was a corral with two horses—a dark one and a light one. They were about to go towards the open gate. A shepherd was there with his herd. To the outer right, two swans were swimming in a pond.

The horses, as well as the shepherd with his herd, were moving towards the left—to the unconscious. A clear in-

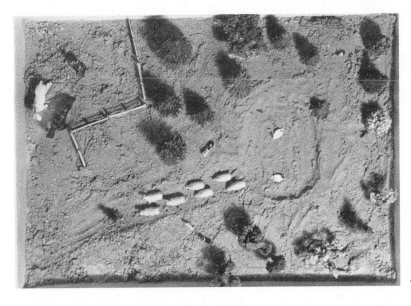

41

troversion was indicated, which James had undergone when he was writing his story, and it was now exerting its effect. The horses were not locked in anymore, as they were in the first picture. They were about to leave their corral and to enter into a relationship with the world. This meant that James had drawn near to his sphere of instinct and had received access, as determined by his nature, to the outside world.

The shepherd probably represented a symbol of Christ, the good shepherd with the sheep.

In the first picture, two ravens were sitting on a barren tree. At that time, one could have easily regarded them as birds of ill omen; i.e., looking at them from their negative aspect. James was an unlucky fellow and had coverd up his melancholic moods about his powerlessness with an emphatically extroverted conduct. Ravens were also friends of the hermits. They were messengers of the gods that brought help to those people living in seclusion. The ravens are also represented in the Bible (Psalms 147:9; Job 38:41) as a kind of bird of God. When in need, the young ravens call to God and are heard by Him.

In his initial picture, James had shown entirely unconsciously, the road to be taken in therapy. In a tribe of Indians in James's native country, a raven symbolizes a bearer of light. The light shines brightest there where darkness is deepest. For this reason, James had to leave this overly rational sphere of consciousness in order to find the light in his inner self that illuminated his creative side.

The swans that now appeared in his picture announced the brighter aspect. Jung mentions, in *Symbols of Transformation,* that "swan" derives from the roots *sven,* the same as "sun" and "sound" and he says swan signifies re-birth and new life. When it embodies as a sunbird, that which is bright and clear, it points also toward an extended consciousness, toward realizing inner possibilities.[19] At the same time, it embodies also a completely different aspect: it has a premonition of what is in the future. When we have a bad feeling, we

[19] C. G. Jung, *Symbols of Transformation,* Collected Works, Vol. 5 (New York: Pantheon Books, Inc., 1967), p. 348.

say: "I have dark forebodings." However, one could not foresee which of the two aspects would be more meaningful.

James worked cheerfully towards his examination. One day he enrolled for the test, not to actually pass it but "to see," as he expressed it, "how much is required." After quite some time, word came that he had passed the examination! The joy was great. Now a college career stood open to him.

However, another question emerged. He had grown accustomed after more than two years abroad to our way of life. How would he feel in his native country? He considered going by freighter, which would take several weeks. Thus he would have time to prepare himself for the future and what might be different awaiting him there.

His parents, who wanted to celebrate what their son had accomplished, decided differently. They sent him a plane ticket; they wanted him to get home as fast as possible!

It was not astonishing that the thought of such a quick transition from one world to the other brought about something like an inner panic. He dreamt: "I was in my native city, in a big house. A fire seemed to have broken out. God was there, but for some reason He could not help. Then the "man in the moon" was called. I saw him as he came from far away out of space. He and God went into a room and held council. What followed was unclear."

The fire that had broken out indicated the inner emotion in James. God by Himself could not help. And yet who was the "man in the moon" who was supposed to assist God? There are endless variations in legends and myths about the "face" in the moon. Man has often been carried off to the moon as punishment. However, a north German legend of a big man who bends at ebbtide to pour water on the earth to put out a fire seemed meaningful to me in this context. As opposed to the glowingly hot ball of the light of day, the moon—with its effect on ebb and flow, embodies the water principle of nature in myths of almost every people.

In a Chinese fairy tale, the man in the moon is mentioned as sitting on the blooming, scented cassia tree. In Africa, the sweet pulp of the cassia is also called manna. Manna was the food sent from the heavens to the Israelites in the desert. It is said to have fallen from heaven at night, at the same time as the dew. Thus, manna is often called bread of the heavens or food of the moon. In the Holy Scriptures, manna is compared with the dew, which in turn was a symbol of prayer. In the Revelation of St. John (2:17), it says, "To him that overcometh will I give to eat of the hidden manna."

In this dream it was again clearly visible how extraordinarily important the encounter of his consciousness with the unconscious was for James. And yet, in a rational manner, this would have been impossible. In having symbolically experienced the Self (which I had to assume had not manifested itself in early childhood) in the birth of Christ, however, a treasure had been granted to James. He not only had at his disposal his ability to learn, but he had also developed a manliness with which he could accomplish the adaptation to the collective. Above all, his soul was now close to God, from whom he could beseech help in prayer. He had already adopted this in everyday life.

One could hope that this experience would alleviate a little the storms that life would also bring to James.

Chapter 7

DEDE:
Conquest of a
Speech Block

Dede came to me for therapy when he was five-and-a-half years old. The events happening during the treatment, which lasted over two years were so varied that it is impossible for me to demonstrate them within the framework of this book. Therefore, I have chosen a few highlights which were of particular importance in the boy's development.

According to the parents' story, Dede's blood heritage had elements from the Caucasians, Kurdistan, Turkey, Crete, Byzantine and Switzerland. This led to many racial, cultural and religious contrasts: native, original ethnic culture, Islam and old and new Christianity. Two maternal ancestors had been stolen as small children from nomad tents, and had been brought up in wealthy Turkish families. The nomads wandering through the steppe lived in eternal feud with their Christian neighbors, but their acts of war were based on a high-level ethics of loyalty towards their own families.

I mention these details because the boy impressd me at once as being very unusual. Willful, yet guileless, eyes looked at me while he leaned against his mother. His vocabulary consisted of a few words, which did not at all coincide with his age. He also exhibited other alarming symptoms. He demanded the presence of his mother all the time, hid within her coat on the street, and wanted to wear a hood (night cap). He had an outspoken preference for blue and refused to wear a pullover of a different color. When he was asked to do something which was against his will, he would tense up. Nothing could persuade him to get into a bathtub. He loved music, and he drew on big pieces of brown paper. It was questionable if he could develop in a normal way.

I found out from the pediatrician how Dede had behaved in the children's hospital where he was treated for an acute staphylococcus infection at the age of 21 months. The experienced woman doctor told me tht Dede's muscles were so tense that a hypodermic needle broke during an injection. For three days, the boy had been in great danger of losing his life. Subsequently, he had recovered relatively fast, but he could neither walk nor talk after his illness. Before his illness, he had seemed to be a healthy child, but now he had to learn these skills all over again. While walking presented no difficulties his speech development lagged far behind the norm.

According to a psychiatric opinion, it was questionable whether he could go to school. This was mainly the reason why the family contacted me.

We spent the first hour together with his brother, who was four years older, in my garden. They played with a cable car so I could observe the boy. Dede directed the course of the game with gestures and a few words. His brother had very little to say.

The first time when Dede came alone to me, he steered straight to my record player, indicating to me that he would like to hear music. Sitting on a low chair, he listened to the music intently. After a while, he motioned me to sit beside him. We listened to Mozart. As the record finished, he said, very satisfied, "green." Then we listened to Bartok. This music, he called "yellow." I realized that these descriptions corresponded to the colored labels in the center of the records. Next he wanted "blue." This was a Bach recording. I watched his intense listening and knew that he had connected the colors with certain composers when he called them green, blue or yellow. We spent several sessions listening to these three composers. I felt that this way, a certain relationship with me had been established, but I knew that I had to try further means for the therapy. Sitting at the piano, I played and sang a children's song. He moved his chair close to me and listened very attentively. I was sure that he did not miss a single sound as he sat motionless in his chair. When I wanted to turn the page and sing a new song, he prevented me very emphatically from doing so. He loved the song concerning the moon, and the picture next to it, with the moon and the stars in the sky. I repeated all verses two or three times. He did not want to hear anything else. Then he closed the book and we went to the playroom on the lower floor. On our way, we passed a gently ticking electric meter. He was startled and grasped my hand. I felt his insecurity and anxiety, and assured him there was nothing to fear.

In the playroom, he went immediately to the sandbox. He built a hill and pierced it on all four sides with his hands, making a tunnel and a hollow space in the center. His face showed me that he did not see anything else but the cave. Then he discovered a candle, which he put inside the cave, and I had to light it. He seemed to like this.

During the following sessions, we were either with the piano or he worked in the sandbox, which he enjoyed. I felt, however, that it was mainly the lights in the cave that fascinated him. He molded the sand very fast and immediately afterward brushed the remaining sand from his hands. Touching the sand seemed to be unpleasant to him.

After some further sessions, Dede's face—originally so serious—brightened. Now he obviously enjoyed coming. When he was picked up after the session, he wanted the door of my house to remain open until he had disappeared—he had to be sure that the house was really open for him. He developed an intimacy with me which he expressed by wanting to sit on my lap while I played the piano, often repeating the "Songs of the Moon." In the meantime, he had discovered a second piece in our songbook entitled "Songs and Sounds for Children's Hearts,"[20] And woe, if I ever skipped a verse! He obviously knew them all after a short while.

One day, he discovered paper and colored pencils. With astonishing firmness he painted a big square. He gave me paper and pencil, indicating that I too should draw my house. When I drew the door, he wanted to see it open. The old chimes beside the entrance also had to be in the picture. This probably gave him the assurance that he could always come back. He began to feel that I understood him. Again and again, he wanted to hear the songs, "Good Moon, You Are Going So Quietly" and "Twinkle, Twinkle, Little Star." Each time, he sat and listened motionless and with great intensity.

I noticed that the boy's hearing was especially acute, for he

---

20 *Sang und Klang furs Kinderhez,* (Berlin: Verlag Neufeld und Henis, 1909).

42

reacted to every little noise. One day, when he was in my office at 11:00 A.M. and the chruch bells were ringing, he became restless, wanting me to open the window so that he could hear them. I drew a church and pointed out the bells in the belfry to him. He then drew my house; besides the door it now also had a dial which he represented by a circle. He tried to draw a bell above it. He did this in a few seconds with one stroke that radiated a tremendous vitality and sureness.

Anything he did was motivated by an inner necessity which left no room for an alternative. His actions were "dedicated" by his unconscious, which hid the problem still in the dark. yet something in him pushed towards the light. This might be the reason why the songs about the moon and the stars that lit up the sky, and also the candle in the sand cave, were so tremendously important. He was not interested in anything else. It would have been utterly useless to try at this time to teach him how to tie his shoes, even though he stumbled over his loose-hanging shoelaces.

Two months later, just before Christmas, I showed Dede an illustration to the song, "Silent Night, Holy Night" in our songbook. There was a brightly lit church, some houses on Christmas night, and people who were walking through fields in deep snow, holding lanterns. I sang and played the Christmas song. Dede listened attentively to the song and also to the story of Christ's birth. He remembered the Christmas tree with many candles. He put a church and a little house [illustration 42] in the sand, arranging them on a little hill. He did not have to make a cave now. To complete the picture, we illuminated the church and the house with electric lights, the kind used in dollhouses. He thoroughly examined the church tower, to see whether it contained any bells, but he did not find any. He was satisifed though, and listened to the church bells ringing at noon each time he was in my house, at which time the window had to be opened. Why was he satisfied our little church had no bells, since he liked the sound so much? Since his vocabulary was still very limited, I learned only later that he was afraid that the church bells could fall down. I had to reassure him again and again that there was a floor under the bell which separated the bells from the rest of the belfry. The bells which let us hear the sound, as it were, between heaven and earth, are a symbol

43

44

of creative energies. His anxiety that the bells should drop down apparently had to do with his fear that he might be overwhelmed by his creative energies with which he could not yet cope. That was why he wanted to be reassured that there would be a floor under the bells as a natural protection. This presented a challenge for me to closely watch his creative utterances and to try to give them direction.

Now Dede liked not only the "Song on the Moon," but he also loved to listen to the Christmas songs with their beautiful pictures of Christmas, as well. Again and again, he put the little house and the church into the sand. Sometimes he added a few more houses to make a little village; or the house stood alone beside the church on the hill. Sometimes he called the house "my house" and at other times that of the Christ child. Very slowly, the mother-child unity—as it gets formed in therapy via the transference—was beginning to dissolve. He felt himself completely accepted and understood, and his Self was protected. He was very secure in "my house" and sometimes that of the Christ child. That he sometimes referred to the house as the dwelling place of the Christ child, was evidence of the impending birth of the divine child—of the manifestation of the boy's Self—as I described it in my introduction.

He began to be preoccupied with more than the Christ child. He also became increasingly interested in churches, for the pictures in our songbook showed the birth of Christ in connection with brightly lit churches. He had already called my house a church. Enthusiastically, we looked at a book with churches and cathedrals. He remembered amazingly well from one time to the next the names of the churches which I had shown him. He even recognized and remembered details of a certain church, because he recalled the rosette pattern of the stained-glass window. He asked me repeatedly to look at the "church book" and finally started to draw and paint churches (illustrations 43 and 44]—no imaginary buildings, but real churches which he had seen either in books or during his excursions into the country. His stroke was not equally sure for drawing churches and cathedrals as it was when he first drew the square. What he could not say in words, he seemed to be able to express much better in drawing and painting. It was noticeable here, too, that an inner need was at work, searching for an expression, as a means of communication. This was so overwhelming at times that the boy's whole being was caught by it. That was probably the reason why no human figures appeared in his play. He was gripped by something very different. Was it possible that the Christian consciousness wanted to manifest itself in him, which for generations had lain dormant in Dede's ancestry? He as fascinated at the sight of churches and by the pictures of the stable in Bethlehem and the divine birth, which he found in our songbook. He was just as intense with drawing and painting his churches.

Christmas passed and another month had gone by. He continued putting the church and the little house into the sand, mostly on top of the hill. Gradually he added other houses and another church—still no people, but two white horses played in the village square*. As seen previously, the white horse often appears in connection with a religious experience. *Two* horses might indicate an impending manifestation.

*For interpretation see pages 92 and 127 cases of James and Marina.

A short time later, Dede built a pretty village on the hill [illustration 45]. It was winter and a little wooden house stood in deep snow, surrounded by snow-covered pine trees with a church right behind. A wedding carriage carrying the queen and king, he said, was drawn up the hill by a white horse and a black horse. Two servants preceded the coach. A great fox seemed to show the way for the wedding procession.

During therapy, we had succeeded in restoring mother-child unity. As already shown, signs had indicated a separation again, since my house was alternately also the house of the Christ child. The Self, symbolized by Christ—the complete, perfected human being—began to detach itself from the mother-child unity. In this picture, the Self was represented as the union of opposites by the wedding of king and queen, and by a carriage drawn by a white horse and a black horse. In interpreting fairy tales, the fox appears when there exists the necessity for a content to become conscious. The writer, Saint Exupéry (*The Little Prince*) also used the fox as the one who teaches what is invisible.[21]

The intensity of his listening to Christmas songs and the ringing of the church bells and the drawing of his churches and cathedrals obviously resulted from the necessary breakthrough, leading to the manifestation of the Self shown by the Christian tradition which had lain dormant in Dede until now. The clever fox—which is the instinct of the boy—were helpful.

Soon afterwards, the ice melted. Dede began to speak normally. He seemed to be reborn. He now discovered other songs in our book. He loved to listen to some particular songs, like "May Renews Everything," or "Come Dear Month of May and Make the Trees Green Again," and to look at the accompanying pictures which showed children at play. But he no longer listened with the same intensity as he had to the song about the moon. He was far more interested in a picture with people in their Sunday outfits walking through sunny fields to church. This picture gave rise to many questions. He wanted to know everything: "Why do people go to church on Sunday? What are they doing in church?" I told him they were listening

21 Antoine de Saint Exupery, *The Little Prince* (New York/London: Harcourt Brace Jovanovich, 1971).

to the stories about God which the minister told them, and that they prayed and sang to the music of an organ.

I went to the piano and tried to improvise the walk to the church and the service: the ringing of the bells, light and heavy sounds, the entrance of the minister, the singing and the organ music. He was immensely fascinated and asked for repeated improvisations, until he finally tried to do the same with his own fingers. It was incredible how his clumsy little fingers labored to find the right keys. And he found them! I wondered whether he had musical talent. He now played the piano with the same intensity as he formerly used to listen to songs. He would not rest until he found the correct tune.

He also wanted to hear stories about God, and he listened attentively when I told him that God cares for all people. "Then he must live on the top floor," he said, "To see all the people."

Since he no longer had difficulties speaking, we discussed the question of his going to school. Normally, he would start school the following year. Throughout his life, Dede had had scarcely any relationship with the outer world. Only under the protection of his caring parents and his older brother had he made any contact with the world. His parents agreed to my suggestion that he go to a private kindergarten two or three times a week, where he would meet other children his own age and where he could get used to them. This attempt only partly succeeded. Dede did not care at all to use his hands for crafts as the other children of his age did. His teacher also had difficulties relating to his intensity. Nevertheless, he did not dislike school and talked about the children.

Meanwhile, a different problem preoccupied him during his visits to my house. One day, while leafing through our songbook, he discovered the picture accompanying a lullaby, "Good Evening, Good Night." I played it for him, but I do not know if he heard it. Steadfastly, he looked at the baby lying in the cradle. I had to assure him that the baby lay in the cradle only during the night. He wanted to know the child's age. I explained to him that only small children sleep in cradles—as soon as they grow older they sleep in beds. I did not sense why he asked me these questions. He listened, and I could see he did hear my answers, but he seemed to be seized by some fear. He was worried that the child would stay in the cradle forever, in spite of my reassurance that he would not.

Instead of churches, he now drew cradles. I understood that he again was living through his forebodings of death, the same ones he had experienced at an early age during his illness. This also might have been the reason why he would not climb into the bathtub. Unconsciously, he feared he would be stuck there. A picture illustrating the song, "Sleep, My Beloved Son," gave him a little consolation. This picture depicted a mother standing beside the cradle, holding her child in her arms. He drew all kinds of cradles for weeks. After trying many times, he even succeeded in painting them in the right perspective [illustration 46].

46

Otherwise, he made good progress. A few months later there was an opening in a municipal kindergarten. An intelligent teacher helped him make the transition to this world by allowing him to draw and paint sitting away from the other children.

During this time, fairy tales appealed to him, especially

47

"Sleeping Beauty." He was engrossed by the idea that the prince wake sleeping beauty from a deep sleep with a kiss. In symbolic language, the fairy tale gave us an insight into Dede's problem: on the one hand, this awakening from a deep sleep also symbolized a rebirth—an awakening to new life. He now drew the glass coffin with Sleeping Beauty and the Prince [illustration 47]. Hopefully, his old problem was slowly being solved so that a new development could begin.

The idea of renewal of life became even stronger when Dede did the next sand picture. He made a broad river, and many people went to bathe in it. He said, "They all dive and then come up to the surface again." Later he expressed it even more distinctively by doing a baptism [illustration 48]. He put a small bowl into the sand and baptized a doll by holding it under water. Man and animals surrounded the ritual in a circle.

We know that Christ's baptism took place by submersion into water. In early Christianity, baptism was a ritual signifying acceptance into the community, and had great significance. The holy water in the church today still has a creative and transforming quality. We recognize from these few samples selected from many others, which we can quote as examples for the submerging into the water, how important this experience was for Dede. A new life could begin and should enable him to slowly obtain the security to confront the outside world.

He developed quite well. Drawing and painting expressed his lively imagination. He could also now play the piano a little. To my astonishment, he would not rest until he could play by ear some of the songs on the piano that I had played. Finally, he was accepted into the first grade at the normal age.

This was the first step in Dede's development which in a sense created a balance between the culture of his ancestors and Christianity. That the whole problem has not yet been cured completely became evident, because his drawings still of Christian churches now included also mosques.

48

Chapter 8

MARINA:
The Background of an
Adopted Child's Inability to Read

Although the small, brown-eyed girl came skipping into my playroom, I could see that she did have rather mixed feelings. Her mother had told her that she could come to me to play. She seemed to be wondering what kind of games these would be. Nevertheless, when she saw the sandbox, she rolled up her sleeves and started to mold the sand. I showed her all the figures she could use for the sand play. With her hands on her hips, she carefully examined the shelves full of figures.

As she stood there with her back to me, I observed her. She had straight, dark hair which fell almost to her shoulders. The weight of her slender, small, child-like figure stood oh her right leg, while the left was a little in front, balanced on the heel and pivoting from left to right. Her slightly dark complexion reminded me of the children from the Mediterranean.

"May I take whatever I like?" she asked.

"Yes, just pick the ones you like best, the ones you would like to play with most," I answered.

She liked a small, wooden house the most, which she put exactly in the middle of the sandbox. She looked at it from all sides and, apparently satisfied, turned back to the figures. She selected some trees as fencing for the grounds belonging to the house. To the left, she built a wooden fence in the shape of a half-circle. This enclosed a grazing place for a white horse that was being cared for by a man cracking a whip. Domestic animals, cows, sheep and geese were grazing near the house and a girl was busy feeding the hens and geese. All these were placed exactly on the left side of the sandbox, while the right stayed completely empty. With her left hand, she made some light furrows in the sand and set a sower in the field who, she said, was sprinkling seeds on the ground [illustration 49].

This picture represented psychological situation which led Marina to be brought to me for observation. Marina had been adopted when she was six weeks old. The adoptive mother had ardently wanted a child. The small girl developed well, although she wet her bed until she was six years old. Once in a while, she showed a strong resistance towards her adoptive parents and would stick obstinately to it. When she was four years old, she wanted a little sister, whereupon her parents adopted a second child. Meanwhile, her parents whose home was in the U.S., had come to Europe. Since they planned to return to America in a few years, a school was chosen where Marina would be taught in her native language. She showed a great deal of talent in drawing and handicrafts, but had problems in arithmetic and reading. Her reading difficulties were so apparent that she required private tutoring already in the second grade. This, however, had not helped her. The adoptive father was particularly unhappy because he had set all his hopes on an intelligent child.

The warm, little, wooden house, which has been a favorite of several children in my practice, at first stood all alone in the center of the sandbox. Did this embody Marina's longing for a warm home, or for inner calm? It could have been a desire for both. The white horse, which grazed somewhat apart from the rest of the life of the farm and yet was held spurred on by the farmer with the long whip, was also meaningful.

The horse, in mythology and folklore, is said to be able to see into the future. It is often described as clairvoyant and clairaudient, and at times, having the capacity to speak. As an animal, it embodies an animalistic level; i.e., a totally unconscious layer in man. As a carrying animal, it is connected to the maternal: being easily frightened connects it to the instinctual world, which cannot be controlled by the conscious.

Another element of the white horse symbol is its religious aspect: in China, a temple was dedicated to the white horse; it is mentioned in the Apocalypse; according to legend, Mohammad was carried by a white horse, Benag, when he ascended to heaven; in ancient religions, the white horse was associated with the sun god.

49

The horse, then represents the unpredictability of nature and, at the same time, that element which aims toward an illumination of consciousness.

In little Marina's sand picture, the white horse was on the very left side. This probably signified, dwelling deep in the child's unconscious, a wounded female-maternal aspect of the little girl, which I hoped to reach. The sower on the right offered a hopeful prognosis as he sowed the seed over the wide field, which would signify fertility.

To the second session, Marina brought a small bouquet of flowers she had picked on the way. When I thanked her, she said, "Isn't that nice? I love you and you love me.

"Today I want to paint," she continued. I showed her the different paints, pencils, pastel chalk and watercolors that were available. I watched, astounded to see the brush strokes she executed with a sure hand, which she then developed into a pretty representation of a blooming tulip. She took the picture home with her to give to her mother.

During the third session, she again occupied herself with the sandbox [illustration 50]. She started by constructing a street across the sand. Then she selected some houses, which she put some distance away from the road. The houses were like those which can be found in our region. In front of them she made a small brook, over which she set a bridge of Oriental structure; next to this, a pagoda; on the water, a junk. Some other Oriental elements—small temples and a white pagoda—were put between the Occidental houses and trees. Large trees were placed on the far left of the growing picture. Shortly thereafter, the street which stretched across the picture, became populated. To do this she picked out, with the greatest care, all the Oriental figures she could find, until a very long train of people seemed to move from right to left. Way up in front, already disappearing into the forest was a Chinese lantern carrier. When I asked little Marina what he was doing in the woods she answered, "He has to bring light into the dark forest." I told her that she was right for I knew that her psyche had started out on the healing path, and I was greatly touched by this. Only through the dark does the path lead to the light. An eternal truth was expressed here, spontaneously coming from the unconscious of the child.

In school, Marina lagged behind because of her inadequate achievement in arithmetic and handwriting. Often she felt excluded from her schoolmates. Perhaps it often felt dark and lonely in her inner self. Symbolically, she had already expressed this in the first picture, when she used the solitary, grazing white horse. Now was the time to find a solution, which would help the child to move out of her inner loneliness.

The third picture told more [illustration 51]. It represented an island that Marina named Hawaii. On the upper left-hand side of the island was a small forest, in front of which was a Hawaiian dancer and some musicians who played while standing in a semicircle before her. A little further below was a small, round pond, crossed by a Chinese bridge, which led to another piece of land, on which only one, little tree stood. This piece of land was surrounded by water. To the right was a completely empty field which could be defined as the mainland.

The whole thing reminded me of a very sad face. For the eyes, which stand for consciousness, there were the foreign musicians with the dancer. On top of that, the forest looked like

50

51

52

a tuft of hair. The small, round pond with the bridge gave me the impression of clenched lips. Here, in my judgment, the whole solitude of the little girl was expressed. What did she want to convey by this? That her mouth was shut, but that she identified herself with the dancer? That she was a child from a far-away country, or that she felt foreign in these surroundings? Both Oriental and Occidental people live peacefully together in Hawaii; therefore, it could be both. That which could not be expressed, because her secret slumbered deep in the unconscious, spoke here for itself. It found expression in an external design. The bare strip of land, which lay nearer to consciousness (on the right side of the picture), was expressing the standstill in Marina's intellectual development. On it, nothing grew; it was uninhabited. And yet in her solitude, which she may have felt because she knew she was adopted, she danced! Involuntarily I remembered the wonderful verse of a Persian poet: "He who knows the power of dance lives in God."

I embraced little Marina for a moment to show her that I understood her language. It was a question of total acceptance of the young girl the way she was.

After this she communicated in many different ways. They

were always artistic, creative, small shapes in clay, color or enamelled. One day, she made a little mast out of clay [illustration 52]. Her artistic capabilities for a child of her age amazed me. And yet, at first I did not know how to interpret the mask. It was a pretty, sharply sculptured, somewhat foreign-looking little face. "It is nothing," she said, but I knew that she liked it too.

After a few weeks, she made another sand picture [illustration 53]. She built a hill in the center and set a church on it; directly in front of it, she placed a Chinese entrance arch. In front of the church, the pathes were divided; the one to the left, down to a small Oriental bridge shaded by blossoming trees, led over a small brook. A little Japanese girl with a parasol was in the middle of the small bridge. The other path went in the opposite direction. It led, in a big curve, to a village with Western houses, which formed an almost complete circle. A whole train of people, the same as those who had been moving toward the forest in the second picture, was nearing the village. A small rickshaw in which a little lady sat, was already entering the village. She was the princess who was going home, commented Marina. To the right, in front, was a small, round pond with fish in it.

East and West were here united in the church with the Oriental entrance. After the child felt that I understood and accepted her secret, the secret could return again with ease to its place in

53

the depths of her being. It seemed to me to be no longer a burden because the little Japanese girl had been represented, in an enchanting way, under the blossoming tree. To be sure, it meant a sacrifice that is always demanded when a new stage of development is reached. An old situation—in this case marked by an Eastern element—recedes into the background to make room for a new one.

Now Marina could attempt to conform to the Western environment. This was expressed in the train of people who, in contrast to the second picture were now moving in the opposite direction, with the princess in the lead, towards the Western-style village. The landscape too, with the little forest of firs, had a Western character. It was as if in the innermost being of the child, East and West had met (as represented by the church with the Oriental entrance arch); as if, just on the basis of this communication, the adaptation to the new surroundings could now take place with great intensity (expressed in the many people). The fish in the pond could be a suggestion of the Self in Christian terms. To be able to attain this, Marina had to sacrifice to some extent a part of herself (the Japanese girl), in order to experience the centering. In the adult, it would mean becoming consciously aware, but the child experiences it in the actual process of making the picture.

In giving a child opportunities with clay, wood, plaster, glass, enamel, colored paper, paints and other materials, I do not expect any artistic masterpieces. Mainly I want to catch hold of the creative energy in the child. I try without any artistic aim, to activate the creative energies that are in danger of being stunted by the daily routine at school and at home. Only in regard to the totality of man can normal development of his capacities be expected. If artistic talents should be aroused in that way, then they will find expression of their own accord. Not until then can the technical side of art be successfully taught. It remains a task of the therapist to discover and encourage any real artistic talent. The same maxim applies to music. For instance, in music, a child may move the keys clumsily with his little fingers; yet, from the intensity and power of formation even in very easy melodies, we can recognize talent, and encourage it. Often it is also a question of developing the child's emotional side and his ability to communicate.

But back to Marina: it was summer, and we often used the sunny hours for playing in the garden. The Self which accompanies the whole process of development can, in my opinion, be supported by the therapist also in playing. Thus, we often played a certain ball game, in which a small ball, thrown by the players to some distant point on the lawn, is the goal. With bigger, colored balls, one tries to come as close as possible to the small one. In this game, I insist that the starting point be changed frequently in order to symbolically engage the different sides of the child which are striving toward a centering.

The play in the sand was nevertheless always attractive, and after awhile, an island picture was re-created [illustration 54]. This time, it showed the same village in which the princess and all her people previously had made their entrance. Here again, were the dancer and the musicians, who livened up the interior space of the village square. Even though the dancer was the only female figure in the representation, the picture gave evidence of a meaningful change in the psyche of the child. Here, it was a circular area in which the dance was performed, a

54

kind of *tenemos,* a protected space, even though located on an island.

For all true freedom, and thus also for the freedom of development, the sense of feeling sheltered is a prerequisite. For this reason, the difference from the first island picture was very great. In the first picture, the dancer seemed abandoned and at the mercy of nature; here, she was under the protection of the man-made village that carried, in its circularly constructed form, the archetypal character of the protector.

The incompletely closed form reminded me in a figurative sense, of the maternal container from which a child is born. The shape of the island brought to mind the uterus and its amniotic fluid, out of which the fruit, the child, is released.

In the *Great Mother,* Neumann states: "The ritual is originally always also dance, in which the body psyche, in the true sense of the word, is set into motion."[22] This picture contained a presentment of the incipient development which was set in motion through the mystery of the dance and in its dynamic.

When little Marina looked at the newly finished picture, she began to dance. She hummed a melody and seemed very happy. Evidently moved, she said, "Sometime I will dance." In the same moment she spotted, through the window, our little daschund, who was walking in the garden. She rushed outside and hugged him. He liked that, for everytime Marina came, she showed him her affection. "He is my friend because he is so fuzzy." He was a soft, long-haired daschund and Marina loved all that was soft and fuzzy. She also loved the rabbits which our neighbor kept. She always wanted to feed them carrots and stroke their soft fur. She would very much have liked to take one home with her.

She began to behave with complete self assurance, was joyful and told me about her adventures. The hours that she spent with me seemed short to her. She often came with a proposal about how she wanted to spend the time. I sensed that she was steadily gaining, slowly but surely, an inner security.

Toward the end of the summer, Marina made a sand picture of the "Birth of Christ" [illustration 55]. The child lay in a

22 Erich Neumann, *The Great Mother* (New York: Pantheon Books, Inc., 1955).

55

cave, surrounded by Mary and Joseph and the shepherds. In front of them, big trees were arranged in a lovely manner, as it to protect the whole event. Instead of the usual three kings of the story, Marina had placed four kings upon galloping horses between two small, completely round hills.

I was very moved by the picture, not only because it was the actual continuation of the preceding one and represented the archetypal birth, but also because the sheer power of it certified the artistic gifts which endowed the child with the capacity to express symbolically that which never could have been expressed verbally. When we think of the forlornness and loneliness which were expressed in the third sand picture, we recognize here, in the symbol of the birth, an expression of a completely new psychic situation.

/ 137

The child was born in the sheltering cave, lovingly surrounded. Symbolically Marina had now assimilated her forlornness. Jung says of the child archetype, in "Child God and Child Hero," *The Archetypes and the Collective Unconscious:* "The various 'child'—fates may be regarded as illustrating the kind of psychic events that occur in the entelechy of genesis of the Self. The 'miraculous birth' tries to depict the way in which this genesis is experienced."[23]

The totality of the small girl's inner experience was further represented in the four kings who were approaching in haste. The collective archetypal aspect that is connected to the regal quality of these figures indicated the union of the interior [cave] and the exterior. This union happens when constellation of the Self comes about. Only on the basis of this numinous, centering experience which resulted from her unity with the therapist in a mother-child relationship, did it now seem possible for Marina to develop her personality and her talents, with which she could exist successfully in this world.

The truly feminine aspect also belonged to her personality, and it seemed to me as though she had represented her two small breasts in the two small hills. She was certainly born to be a mother, and she often spoke of how she would one day marry and have children. How right she was!

During the therapy hours, an intense effort was made to strengthen further her newly gained personality. The new aspects were as tender as new grass which had just sprouted out of the ground. Marina turned with renewed ardour to artistic handicrafts: a figure of a small girl was poured out of plaster, and pretty little pieces of jewelry were made out of enamel. Most of them, she gave to her mother and friends.

At this point, the problem of school reappeared. In languages, and particularly in spelling, she had made no great progress so far; the time at our disposal had really been too short. She had had therapeutic sessions twice a week for only four months. Marina's father still had strong doubts regarding her intelligence, while the second child, almost five years old and also adopted, made a very clever impression.

[23]C. G. Jung, *The Archetypes and the Collective Unconscious,* Collected Works, Vol. 9 (New York: Pantheon Books, Inc., 1959), p. 166.

We decided to engage a tutor who used a method suited to help Marina overcome her difficulties with reading and writing. Marina wrote almost daily, under her tutor's guidance, a short composition about her daily adventures. The words that she didn't know, or whose spelling was difficult, were written especially large and clear on a piece of paper, arranged in alphabetical order. This way, her own little spelling book was produced, from which Marina could learn words unknown to her, and look up once more those which she had forgotten. Her compositions were short at first, consisting only of short, simple sentences. The tutor then typed out each composition and Marina made a pretty drawing to go with each one. Each sheet was carefully put into a ringed notebook, so that gradually a book of colorful stories and illustrations was made.

Marina began to show great zeal in writing and reading. Each composition gave more information about her psychic development. After the seventh hour of tutoring, she made visible progress in reading; the following night, she dreamt that she was the best pupil in her class. She prayed to God that He might help her. The spontaneous, religious experience that was so impressively represented in the birth of Christ seemed to deepen in

56

still another way. Marina formed a face out of clay that resembled Christ [illustration 56]. If we remember the face she had formed four months before, about which she did not want to say anything, and then look at this new face, the change that had taken place in her inner Self can clearly be seen. The small figure had the features of a Mexican mask, while the new face showed the calm expression of Christ. Hopefully, Marina would eventually succeed in completely losing her inner unrest, which she expressed from time to time. One day, when her little sister had had a strong reaction to a vaccination, Marina wore a sling made of her mother's silk shawl. It was again and again necessary for her to get special attention, for life was not easy for her. Her father, although constantly reassured by me, did not want to believe that Marina's intelligence was average. He had insisted that she read aloud to him, which was obviously hard for her. To read to the tutor, where she and her weakness were accepted, was considerably easier, and there she showed constant progress. After two months of tutoring, the great moment came when Marina could read everything that her father placed in front of her without mistakes. Her father, touched by his long desired event, at once gave a family party in order to properly celebrate this moment.

Here we recognize one of the motives that can lead to difficulties in the relationship between adoptive parents and children. Parents often imagine a set of pictures of the much-wanted child, and great problems arise when the child does not correspond to this image. Disillusionment on both sides is usually the result. Special empathy is required by the therapist, along with the ability to imagine himself to be in the environment and thought processes of both parties. It is a matter of reconciling opposites which we are striving for within the confines of therapy, which also includes parents and children.

Marina showed real improvement. The parents decided, therefore—too early in my judgment—that Marina should go to school in her native country, since they themselves intended to return to America in the near future.

Shortly before her departure, I asked Marina to make another sand picture hoping it might perhaps afford me an insight into what impression the parents' sudden decision had made on Marina.

57

Again there was an island [illustration 57]. This time it was a mountain which was crowned by a strong, compact fortress with enclosed walls. The tower in the courtyard was not a lookout tower, as in most fortresses. It was important to Marina that it belonged to the castle's chapel. Trees and blossoming bushes surrounded the fortress. In front of it, outside and in the open, stood a girl dressed in white. Below next to the bridge that made the connection to the main island, a strong man stood on guard. A small ship lay at anchor.

In the early Middle Ages, fortresses and castles were built mostly on lofty heights. They afforded protection; behind the enormously thick walls, life and property were secured. When I asked who lived in this castle, Marina answered, "Mary." Since Marina had depicted the birth of Christ a few weeks earlier, it was almost possible to assume that the child sensed Mary, the mother of God, the archetypal mother: the mother who had as innocently as the little girl, conceived, and who, as the mother of Christ, became the essence of maternal security. It was the protection that Marina had obtained by herself. It was her own fortress that stood there; behind those walls she could protect her newly acquired possessions from intruders. It was her inner security that could be felt here and which she did not want to surrender anymore. A guardian should decide to whom entrance to the fortress would be given.

This made it possible for me to hope that nine-year-old Marina was secure enough to face the new, still unknown, circumstances of life with no help from another.

The whole process of Marina's psychic development reminded me of the French fairy tale in which a white mare had been helpful to a young man in mastering difficult tasks necessary to win the princess. When we invited the horse to his wedding, it appeared in the shape of Mary—a surprising parallel to the case described here.

Chapter 9

A Twenty-Three-Year Old Woman: Restoring a Weak Ego

The initial picture [illustration 58] by a 23-year-old woman was done during a session of one-and-a-half hours, while she was in a very depressed mood. These moods were the reason for consulting me. Any verbalization of the situation at the beginning appeared to me inopportune. Therefore, I proposed sandplay, which affords direct access to man's deeper, more primitive levels.

The picture represents the symbol of the feminine and of the masculine: uterus and phallus lie side by side. Connected to them is a circle from which a point is directed toward the upper right. The whole, reminiscent of an embryo, represents a complete expression of an unconscious sense of the opposites as they are experienced in early childhood, with the distinct tendency toward their union in the Self.

From the young woman's contact with the sand, there grew the need to work in clay. Thus, three days later, a figure was produced that showed a witch holding in her arm a waning sickle of the moon. She represented the archetypal negative mother, whose conquest is symbolized by the waning moon [illustration 59].

Two days later, another sand picture was made [illustration 60]. Out of a half-moon grew a tree. It represented the Self with its powers of growth and the union of opposites: the trunk embodied the male principle; the crown, the female principle.

Two days later, a Christ figure holding a crescent moon in his arm [illustration 61] was produced from clay. The Self is represented here as *imago dei*. It contains the basis for a further development, represented in the new moon as the point of new female life.

This new life was produced impressively in another representation [illustration 62]: it showed a monk holding in his arm a newborn girl.

Because of her concern with the deeper levels of her psyche, the young woman experienced a rebirth in the unconscious. Only then was her own masculine component positively indicated. This is shown in the figures of "The Prince" [illustration 63], "The Primitive" [illustration 64], and finally, "A Boy" [illustration 65]. The figures, produced in quick succession, were an anticipation of the ensuing analysis, which consisted in bringing to consciousness and integrating very abundant dream material. During this time, the critical moment of the developmental disturbance was also uncovered.

This was expressed in a drawing which the young woman had made as a three-year-old child, and which she called a representation of man. On my request, the drawing was reproduced from memory [illustration 66]. It represents a urinating and defecating child, as depicted by four circles. This representation amounted to experiencing the totality of man, who also has a dark side.

Inasmuch as our present culture represses the dark side of our existence, the drawing had been called indecent by the girl's mother and torn up before her eyes. Thus, the manifestation of the Self had been destroyed. It was restored in the ensuing analysis, and shows up well in the form of two successive mandalas in the sandbox in three-dimensional shape [illustration 67 and 68].

58

59

60

61

62

63

64

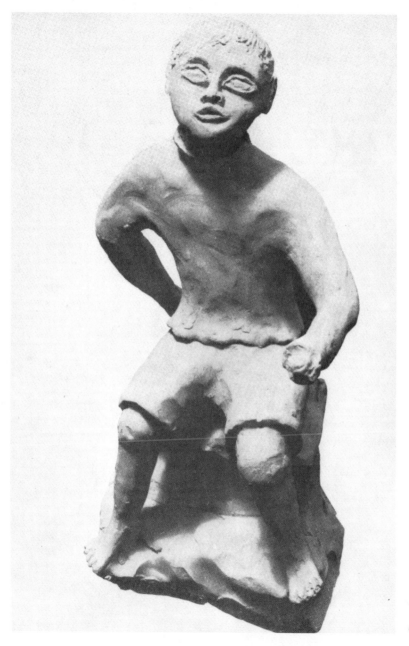

65

66

67

68

Chapter 10

A Young Man:
Religious Background
in the Case of Blushing

Illustration 69 is the initial picture of a young man, 25 years of age. He asked for an appointment with me because he suffered from annoying blushing. This serious handicap in his contact with other people hindered his development; neither could he make a decision as to what profession to choose. A previous verbal analysis did not bring about the desired result. Now he hoped to get some help from sandplay therapy.

He looked at the figures, but they did not appeal to him. Instead, he started to build a square in mosaics in the sandbox, using different shades of blue. I was struck by the predominance of the color blue; only a few red mosaics near the center and two single yellow ones toward the left were noticeable. It occurred to me to ask him what yellow meant to him. After a short reflection, he answered, "The Jews had to wear a visible yellow star on their clothing during the persecution." This answer came so quickly that I deduced from it that the young man was basically preoccupied with a religious problem. This idea was supported by the prevailing blue color in the mosaic. Blue is the color of the sky; it is also the color of Mary's heavenly coat. For this reason, blue is often interpreted as a symbol of Christian religion. Could there be a Christian-Jewish problem present here? I asked myself.

For the second expression in the sandbox [illustration 70], he used some figures: palms, a straw hut, animals, a dark woman dancer, and some Negro children. This was pointed toward some region in Africa, an area often called the Dark Continent. From this, I concluded that his problem seemed to be still in the unconscious. The black dancer also indicated a side of him that remained hidden.

The feminine part of being, immanent to the masculine, was initially experienced through the mother and was therefore the elementary character of the maternal. In the growing boy, its character changes and corresponds to the figure which Jung calls the *anima*. The anima unconsciously accompanies the development of the masculine; as the name says: "she animates the development.'" So we can recognize in this dancer as the anima which motivates the development of the young man.

It was striking that all animals in his sandplay production appeared in couples. The number two symoblized the contrast of, as well as the tendency to connect, polarities. Plato spoke of "the one and the other."

The third illustration [71] led to an excavation site. Archaeologists were about to uncover precious floors: squares of golden shimmering stones. A wanderer, carrying his bundle on his shoulder, was about to walk from the left lower corner toward the uncovered precious stones. The wanderer stands for a person who is searching in vain for his home in the outer surroundings, because he can find it only inside himself. There was no doubt that the young man was a wanderer, too, searching for, and attempting to restore, a lost relationship with his roots and his ancestors. Judging by his pictures, I concluded his roots were in the Near East, and were in the process of being uncovered.

He told me that he had spent some time as a young Jewish boy in a monastery, in order to be protected from persecutions. In this connection, he remembered a dream which he had had recently. He said, "In the newspaper is written: 'missing: myself'."

In his early youth he could not live according to his tradition, nor had he ever experienced the security of the maternal.

As mentioned in the introduction, it is my opinion that disturbances like these in early childhood prevent the constellation of a centering which would lead to the development of a healthy ego. Having lost his mother, his longing to be cared for by the maternal became overly strong and prevented a normal development. The dream shows that under these circumstances his ego consciousness had not been formed.

In the next production [illustration 72], he built a hill upon which a tree grew. Beside it, he said, stood the Jew. All kinds of

69

70

71

72

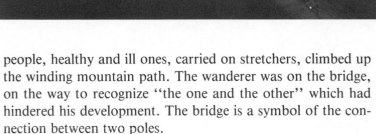

people, healthy and ill ones, carried on stretchers, climbed up the winding mountain path. The wanderer was on the bridge, on the way to recognize "the one and the other" which had hindered his development. The bridge is a symbol of the connection between two poles.

Sacred places have been announced since olden times by trees located on elevated places. The Jew who makes a pilgrimage to Jerusalem says he is "walking up the mountain." This mountain symbolized the Jewish homeland.

This young man was fulfilling the task set by his fate. He was the wanderer who joined all the other wanderers who walked up the winding path of the mountain. He shared his fate with all the other people, because *every* human being has to find the way to himself. This path leads by way of the experience of the divine, in which everybody participates. Since the Middle Ages, the one-sided, rational way of thinking, through buffets of fate, war and precarious conditions (being exiled from the homeland), has blocked off many people from having a relationship to religion. The oneness with God is denied them. They are all searching for the approach, which is closed against them, to this goal that is so buried in the unconscious.

Behind the hill, children were playing and the same dark dancer was dancing. The young man called these scenes paradisiacal, while previously the dancer has been moving in the midst of a situation of conflict [illustration 70].

From illustration we can see the young man's development. He was on the path that all must go, to bring about individuality.

After the creation of this picture, we discussed the possibility of his making a trip to Israel. It seemed to me that this trip would be of help in his psychic development. Even though no money was available, a "chance encounter" resulted in an invitation to visit Israel.

Before leaving, he did another sand picture [illustration 73]. He called it "The Garden of Eden." It is centered and enclosed, and yet there is a gate leading to a small, artistically constructed temple. A magic peace and quietness radiates from this picture.

The union of "the one and the other" appeared in his seeking an archetypal way to this sanctuary. The blue and yellow colors were divided rather regularly and led from the periphery to the sanctuary in the center. We know of the ritual path of worshipping the deity or a sanctuary from many ancient cultures (Egypt, Babylon). To this day, the Catholic faith has kept alive the procession as a ritual leading to transformation.

Here, it is a question of experiencing the Self: reaching the treasure hidden inside him.

What had appeared in the second picture as only a hint — the union of the religious opposites and the transformation of the dark anima — was now ready to be realized in a ritual. The archetypal, collective anima — the princess — danced in the little temple.

Many cultures use dance as a ritual to worship their gods. Only then, touched and moved by the divine, does this soul become active in him. The anima is said to set in motion the free, creative impulse in man. She brings about true freedom, for which security is a prerequisite.

The small temple and the paradise-like quietness pouring forth from the garden assured him this security. According to my experience, the anima appears in the sand picture either at the same time of, or immediately after, the centering. The anima was now visible. As she manifested herself in this picture, new aspects of ego growth could be expected. As I mentioned in my introduction, this becomes apparent following the centering. Until now, his ego could not grow positively, because the dissolution of the mother-child unity and deprivation of security within the maternal made this impossible.

In Israel, the young man dreamed: he was looking at people who were close to a fiery volcano, and saw their skin hanging in shreds.

The skin-shedding of the snake is a similar image, symbolizing transformation and renewal. In alchemy, the change takes place in the hot fire. A renewed vitality is often depicted as fire. This experience, laden with significance, often is accompanied by strong emotions when it is brought into consciousness.

The actual meeting of the "other," with Israel, let him experience the process of change, which led to the manifestation of the Self. He had expressed this intuitively in his sandplay. He now was able to look at the world in a new way.

After his return from Israel he had another dream, in which he found a newborn baby under the branches of a great tree in a park. The child symbolized this newly acquired outlook on life (*Weltanschauung*). This was expressed in his no longer having to choose the "one *or* the other;" he could now live with one *and* the other, now that he had experienced both.

The next sand picture [illustration 74], which is a desert landscape with animals, demonstrated his landing in Israel, he said. Looking closely, I saw that the hills in the picture had the shape of a woman. She lay in the water with pulled-up knees like an embryo. This was probably his personal anima who was born from the earth—i.e., out of the unconscious—at the moment when he touched the earth of his heritage. The animals of the steppe pointed to the instinctual region in the unconscious. After Self manifestation, the anima was, like the ego, still on a primitive level.

With this act, a circle had been closed. The circle's point of origin had lain in the inner birth. His blushing disappeared, and soon he was offered a job which solved his professional problem and delineated a path to the future. Energies were released and could be used for this new activity. The newly awakened energies were represented in illustration 75 in another wide, tree-lined path. It contained many other colors besides blue and yellow, and led to a fruit-bearing tree. The fountain of new life was symbolized by a well, from which a colorful path led to the wide, big road. Beside the well sat a female figure, the feminine aspect of his own being; he could not have accomplished his creative work without help.

Here, the tree was the symbol for that which grows out of the earth and unites in itself the masculine and the feminine, which corresponds to the growth and fertility of life.

74

75

EPILOG

I have chosen some cases from my practice and tried to show how an unbearable block in the psychic development of a child or an adolescent can be released, allowing him to grow normally again. It is mostly of no avail to treat such an arrested development with reason alone. We must try to understand the symbolic language with which the many-sided psyche expresses itself in images and dreams. Thus, we can reach the psyche's creative seeds which are able to effect a transformation and change in a child's relationship to life.

In all cases presented here, it was possible, sooner or later, to reach the higher developmental stage which was usually hinted at symbolically in the patient's first picture. I could mention many more examples, but I want to show only a few typical processes.

Occasionally, situations were encounters where the expected cure was not achieved, because it can happen that we do not succeed to bring about a new order of the energies in the course of therapy. When dealing with such irrational events—as presented by the psychic phenomena which are based on a hidden process—it is often very difficult for the parents of troubled children to have the necessary understanding and patients to wait for a complete cure. This is especially the case if, after a short time, signs of improvement become evident.

The course of psychic development could be best compared with flowing water. A commentary in the I Ching says:

> *It flows on and on, merely filling at the places it traverses; it does not shy away from any dangerous place, nor from any sudden plunge; nothing can make it lose its*

own intrinsic essence. It remains true to itself in all cir-
cumstances. Thus, truthfulness in difficult conditions will
bring about the penetration of a situation within one's
heart. And once a situation is mastered from within the
heart, the success of our exterior actions will come about
all by itself.

When we succeed with this work, of bringing about an inner
harmony which defines a personality, we can talk of grace.

BIBLIOGRAPHY

Michael Fordham, *The Life of Childhood* (London: Kegan Paul, Trench, Trubner & Co., Ltd., 1944).

Yu-Lan Fung, *History of Chinese Philosophy* (Princeton: Princeton University Press, 1952).

Handwörterbuch des deutschen Aberglaubens, Vol. 20 (Berlin: de Gruyter).

E. Humperdink, *Sang und Klang furs Kinderherz* (Berlin: Neufeld & Henius, 1911).

J. Huzinga, *Homo Ludens,* Rowohlts Encyclopedia, Vol. 21.

I Ching or *The Book of Changes.* The German translation by Richard Wilhelm. Renderd into English by Cary F. Baynes. Bolligen Series XIX (Princeton: Princeton University Press, 1968).

Carl Gustave Jung, *Psychological Types,* Collected Works, Vol. 6 (New York: Pantheon Books, Inc., 1954).

      The Development of Personality, Child Development and Education," Collected Works, Vol. 17 (New York: Pantehon Books, Inc., 1954).

      & Karl Kerenyi, *Essays on a Science of Mythology,* Bolligen Series XXII (Princeton Unversity Press, 1969).

Finlay Mackenzie, *Chinese Art* (London: Spring Books, 1961).

W. Nigg, *Grosse Heilige,* "The Saint in Protestantism: Gerhard Tersteegen" (Zurich: Artemis, 1946).

Nancy W. Ross, *The World of Zen* (New York: Random-House, Inc., 1960).

Richard Wilhelm & Eugen Diederichs (translators), *Chinesische Märchen* (Jena, 1927).

SIGO PRESS

SIGO PRESS is a publishing firm specializing in Jungian related works with an appreciation for its content and its audience.

OTHER BOOKS AVAILABLE

PUER AETERNUS   Marie-Louise von Franz

A study of the positive and negative qualities of the *Puer Aeternus*, the eternal youth and creative child within us. This book includes an indepth interpretation of Saint Exupéry's *The Little Prince*.

ENCOUNTERS WITH THE SOUL: Active Imagination
as Developed by C. G. Jung   Barbara Hannah

Active Imagination is thought to be *the* most powerful tool in Jungian psychology for achieving wholeness. Barbara Hannah in her book *Encounters With the Soul* illustrates step by step this important method of reaching the unconscious.

SIGO PRESS
2601 Ocean Park Blvd., #210
Santa Monica, CA. 90405

S I G O PRESS

ORDER FORM

2601 Ocean Park Boulevard 210
Santa Monica, CA 90405
213 471-1003

NAME		
ADDRESS		
CITY	STATE	ZIP

DATE

QUAN	DESCRIPTION		LIST PRICE	AMOUNT
	SANDPLAY *D. Kalff*	paper	$11.50	
	PUER AETERNUS *M.L. v. Franz*	paper	9.00	
		hardcover	14.50	
	ENCOUNTERS WITH THE	paper	9.50	
	SOUL *B. Hannah*	hardcover	15.00	

SUBTOTAL	
CALIFORNIA SALES TAX	
SHIPPING & HANDLING	
TOTAL	

Shipping and handling costs:
add $1.50 for the first book and .15 for
each additional book.
California Residents Add 6% Sales Tax.

All books shipped via Book Post unless otherwise specified. Books will be shipped upon receipt of payment. Sorry, no COD.

Bookstores and wholesalers are allowed trade discounts. Credit applications and discount schedule available upon request.